Draft 141

Incomplete without surface noise

The world is not yet clothed in garments which befit it; in architecture, furniture, clothes, we are still using and wearing things which have no real relation to the spirit which moves our life. We are wearing and using them simply because we are accustomed to them. The intellectual excitement which moves individual designers does not affect the mass of people.

— Eric Gill, *An Essay on Typography*

Most people shrink in fear from the task of designing their surroundings. They are afraid that they will make foolish mistakes, afraid that people will laugh at them, afraid that they will do something "in bad taste." And the fear is justified. Once people withdraw from the normal everyday experience of building ... they are literally no longer able to make good decisions about their surroundings, because they no longer know what really matters, and what doesn't.

— Christopher Alexander, *The Timeless Way of Building*

One day Soshi was walking on the bank of a river with a friend. "How delightfully the fishes are enjoying themselves in the water!" exclaimed Soshi.

His friend spake to him thus: "You are not a fish; how do you know that the fishes are enjoying themselves?"

"You are not myself," returned Soshi; "how do you know that I do not know that the fishes are enjoying themselves?"

— Kakuzo Okakura, *The Book of Tea*

Cadence

& Slang

Cadence & Slang
by Nick Disabato

Written in Chicago between 2008 and 2010.
Printed in Ann Arbor by Sheridan Books in 2010.

ISBN: 978-0-615-34171-2
Library of Congress Control Number: 2010934252

All errata pertaining to this edition are listed at http://cadence.cc/errata/.

All URLs were sourced at the time of this book's publication. However, the web's dual blessing and curse is that it's ephemeral: content dies, or sites point users to different locations. If you find a dead link that's not yet listed on the above errata page, please email the author.

Say hello:
nickd@nickd.org

Learn more:
http://nickd.org
http://cadence.cc

Slang is the vernacular change of what we once knew.

Cadence is the rhythm that we apply to what we understand.

For Mom, Dad, Elena, and Erin.

Introduction

The first time I used a computer, I was two years old. Six years later, I built my first computer from scrap parts. (It didn't work.) In the ten years that followed, I learned a bunch of things that could only qualify as "power user:" command line prompts, tweaking BIOS settings, applying the "Hot Dog Stand" theme to Windows 3.11, overclocking a computer with an air conditioner, setting a motherboard on fire.

But around 2002, my mindset began to change. As I worked all-nighters in college, I cared more about how easy it was to complete tasks than I did about tweaking the details of my hardware and software. A natural progression followed: I became interested in usability. I paid more attention to the details of layout. I tried to think about what I was thinking as I became familiar with something new.

At the same time, lots of products were being released that focused more on experience than features. They were tremendously successful, both in sales and in educating users about what to expect out of humane, useful technology. And now we're trying to reverse engineer them. What qualities of successful products made them successful? What craft comes into play?

THE BEGINNING.

The history of manufactured products pivots around the Industrial Revolution, circa 1850. During this time, mass production of consumer goods shifted away from personal and craftsmanlike methods of production. Prior to this, the creators of most manufactured goods were intimately connected with their consumers. Mass production presented a trade-off: increased output of more products, but the loss of a solid manufacturer-consumer relationship, degraded worker conditions, and products that were often second-rate. Quality and kindness competed with companies' financial success. Now there's an incentive to do only good enough.

Of course, many technological products (e.g. computers, cell phones, and cameras) would be infeasible without the inventions and attitudes that took root in this period. But "good enough" conflicts with consumers' desire for well-managed, humane experiences. In the past ten years, new products have addressed the problem by providing better service, simpler functionality, and improved clarity – and they've done so with more financial success than those that neglect such attention. Consumers are willing to pay a premium for quality: they understand that in technology, as in much of life, you get what you pay for.

And so.

This book is about interaction design, which is the art and craft of making things easier to use. Useful things make more sense to people. They add beauty and simplicity to our lives.

Technology is reductive by definition. It connects with our lives by metaphor, with an internal slang that has to be translated during its use.

The best technology is alive and humane. It treats you well. It listens. It responds in a way that makes sense. It apologizes when it screws up. It rejoices when you do well. In short, it's built to act like an empathetic and supportive person.

When a product fails, we believe that its bad behavior is *our* fault, that it's a quirk we must endure in order to complete the task. For better or worse, this impression could not be further from the truth. Human beings made this problem – and we have the power to fix it. We can connect the experiences of people in the real world to the native slang of a mechanical world. We can grudge machines' foibles, or we can try to change them so they act like supportive colleagues.

Well-executed designs are easier for users to learn. It's easier for them to finish tasks. And the cadence that users' work attains will be dramatically more fulfilling than they had ever known.

How to do it.

Good interactions involve more craft than art, which sets our field apart from other areas of design. Interaction designers cultivate a sensitivity to the issues, common and uncommon, that can make technology more difficult and frustrating. Moving that button to the right location – and making it look like a button. Cutting out that redundant paragraph of help text. Changing the layout of a web page to make it easier to read. These decisions are more functional than aesthetic, a fact that recalls the famous statement of Apple founder Steve Jobs: *design is how it works*. Once you understand what problems affect a product's usability and why, they're easy to see. All it takes is practice at being perceptive.

Rob Walker, "The Guts of a New Machine," New York Times, November 30, 2003. See also: http://www.nytimes.com/2003/11/30/magazine/the-guts-of-a-new-machine.html?pagewanted=all

So this book isn't limited to those who self-identify as interaction designers or usability analysts – in fact, seasoned interaction designers may find a lot of the content to be obvious, as very few new ideas are advanced.

These problems affect everyone in our field, though, because we all make design decisions, sometimes unconsciously, every day, and they have to result in something that our customers won't want to jettison into the sun. If you're a graphic designer or software engineer, and you want to understand the basics, the starting point: you've come to the right place. And if you think that writing code, building circuits, running a data center, or promoting strategy excludes you from that, ask yourself: who are you working for?

WHAT'S WRITTEN AFTER THIS PAGE.

This book offers a series of principles for building useful, practical, and humane technology. It's organized into seven chapters that address the problems facing interaction design, and how designers can adapt and respond to them.

Ultimately, it should teach you how to frame any new project, and how to revise a current product so it's easier to use. My hope is that in confronting these problems, we can push ourselves to change our attitudes, question our premises, and make something better in this world.

The first half of the book covers the unique slang in which technology can communicate, and suggests how to make products that can better adapt to us.

The second half discusses the way that we perceive technology, and the ideal cadence that we adopt when we're deeply immersed in productive activity.

Slang:

Successful products are confident, empathetic, and kind.
In technology:
- Consumers drive progress more significantly than corporate customers.
- Utility and simplicity encourage adoption more than style.
- Forgiving interfaces cause less frustration, helping users adopt a positive, stronger relationship with the product.

1:
Empathy & Kindness

1.1. *Never lose sight of what you believe in.*

Products reflect the values and desires of their creators - and those with sincere interest in design, and attention to its details, tend to make better designed things. It takes hellbent resolve to design well. It's not enough to say you want good design: you have to love it and demand it.

Your attitudes come from your beliefs about what constitutes beauty and quality. You probably formulated these early in your career. Don't forget them. Write them down; post them someplace ridiculously conspicuous. They'll keep you on track during times of confusion and uncertainty.

1.2. *Design on your own terms.*

Many great products represent some demonstrable improvement on what once existed. This can take many forms: simplicity, features, speed, or finding a new way to do an old thing. At the same time, we design based on what we know, and it's hard to realize totally novel possibilities. In technology, there's a fine line between inspiration and rote copying.

Because our field progresses so fast, it's hard to find the time for inspiration. So many designers take the easier route: looking at what already works, and copying those designs with slight modifications. In technology, there are leaders who figure out ways to advance the medium and make existing things more useful; and there are followers, who borrow from the leaders to make what they believe are safer bets.

Copying is now so frequent that great products which do new things have become the exception, not the rule. But copies neglect the subtler features of successful products. For example, music players copied the iPod between 2002 and 2007, but ignored the integration with iTunes, and placed less emphasis on perfecting such a connection.

The interplay between leaders and followers is reminiscent of the "cargo cults" that appeared after World War II. During the war, the United States and Japan shipped supplies to small

Pacific Island nations that served as slapdash bases. Runways were built to accommodate the airplanes.

Once the war ended, there was no more use for the bases, so the Americans and the Japanese left. But the isolated societies were fascinated by this new technology, and they built runways of their own, complete with air traffic control, ground crews, and so on. "Airplanes" were built out of straw. But the real airplanes never landed. They had perfectly emulated the whole pomp and circumstance of an airplane's arrival, for aircraft that would never appear.

The systems necessary to build, fly, and land an airplane were missing. The entire *context* was ignored. The operation had no integrity. None of the engineering and infrastructure problems were addressed. And why not?

1.3. *Design interactions like you're typesetting writing.*

Interactions are narratives. Hopefully, interactions augment the stories of users' lives in a beneficial and constructive way. Can you think of anything you've used that accomplishes this? Or can you think of something that you wish did so, but failed in some way? *What* way? What would bridge that gap?

Writing is the art of communicating ideas, and typography is the art of displaying those ideas in a clear and readable way. When it functions well, typography can improve writing, communicating with equal importance. In the 20th century, many influential authors - David Foster Wallace, Richard Brautigan, e.e. cummings - used inventive typography to their advantage.

In an email client, for example, one task is to reply to an existing message. Another task is to compose an email from scratch.

Returning to interaction design, a **task** is a user's perceived goal. In order to communicate this goal, the user works with an **interface**, which is the surface appearance of a product: its buttons, menus, text fields, and so on.

Writing is to typography as tasks are to interfaces. Users communicate their tasks to the interface as input, and the product's job is to interpret and respond to that input. The separation between a task and an interface is similar to the difference between ideation and execution in writing and typography. It's up to the interaction designer to provide calmness and balance to the resident slang.

1.4. *Write a mission statement.*

Before you can make anything, you have to determine what you want to make. How do you build consensus with other team members?

A **mission statement** begins this process by concisely answering the most basic questions: what you do, for whom you're doing it, and why. As with any big question in life, it shouldn't be taken lightly or composed in a vacuum. Develop it into something substantial and satisfying. This provides consensus on broad matters and guides you though ambiguous times. Refer to the mission statement in the development process, to determine which decisions fulfill it *and why*.

1.5. *Take the time to get it right.*

The beginning of any product is stressful, and it's easy to make mistakes without noticing. Stopgap solutions pervade products that weren't designed well early on; but in technology, it's impossible to build well on a shoddy foundation. The patchwork of fixes is untenable in the long term, because they require exponentially more effort to fix.

Furthermore, the *first* product in its class is rarely the *best* one. Early releases are overshadowed by those who took the extra time to make a product easier and more enjoyable to use.

Also, releasing too quickly risks more mistakes. The earlier that mistakes are made, the more damaging they can be, because new features may be built on shaky foundations. Such faults can spread epidemically and take over new versions of the product. Solutions that work *well enough* aren't the same as solutions that work *well*.

It's easier to discard initial failure and start anew than it is to fix every part of a large project. But even then, we take away some knowledge of how to do it right the next time.

1.6. *Products should be fast and reliable.*

A product is only as good as the code and hardware that powers it. Nobody wants to use something that's buggy or unreliable. While it sometimes helps to slow the user down to ensure a lack of error, they should always feel a sense of accomplishment in what they're doing. Any cognitive interruption is problematic, and any unintentional data loss is disastrous.

For more on cognitive interruptions, see 6.1.

Performance sacrifices are unacceptable; readable, beautiful code is less ideal than a perceptibly fast product. Steven Frank, cofounder of Mac software company Panic, emphasizes this:

It's not just that the iPhone has fancy woo-woo transitions and purty graphics; [its quality] runs all the way down the software stack. For example, when I tap on something, I don't have to hover

Steven Frank, untitled, stevenf. com, http://stevenf.tumblr. com/post/218293148/a-couple-people-have-asked-me-to-post-an-update

for five seconds wondering "now did it get that tap, or do I have to do it again?" This is something other platforms are still struggling with. When we say you have a bad experience, this is the sort of thing we mean. It has little to do with features, and everything to do with core functionality.

An interface's appearance matters, of course, but so does its **behavior** - which is the way that products respond to user input.

Performance is behavior. When we talk about good interactions, we should focus as much on the way that something is coded as the way that it looks. For example, the quality of search results matters just as much as how they're displayed. A form's validation mechanisms matter just as much as its layout. And the algorithms that comprise an online store's recommendation engine matter just as much as how those recommendations are presented.

A beautiful concept with poor technical execution remains unfinished, one that never came alive from sketches on a white board. Focus on both ends; concepts matter less than their execution.

1.7. Develop for intermediate users.

Let's consider three broad experience levels: beginners, intermediates, and experts. These three levels apply to all products, and their exact boundaries vary from product to product. A user's experience level depends on how many features he uses, how easily and quickly he works with those features, how extensively he customizes the product, and how willing he is to try out new tools.

Beginners have rarely or never worked with a given kind of product. They likely have no experience - or only limited experience - with your interaction model. They haven't figured out how to work with your product *or anything else like your product*. If they do have any experience with similar technology, they have little to no substantial productive output on it.

Experts are exactly the opposite, of course. They know most of a product's features, love figuring out new things, and likely have passionate opinions about their favorite tools. They have substantial experience both with using a specific product, and in technology at large. They know what makes a product good and what makes a product bad *for them*, and they can articulate why. They have almost no trouble figuring out new products.

Intermediates are the hardest group to describe. They represent a broad range of experience levels and they work with a wide range of products. They have passing fluency with whatever products they choose to use. They tend to adopt routines around these products, and are more hesitant to embrace new ones unless prompted by circumstances or people they know. They know all of the basic functions of a product, and they learn more advanced features when they provide an essential benefit.

Beginners and experts each represent minority segments. In many situations, designing for intermediates will please most potential customers. It's easiest to prove this by showing why you shouldn't target either beginners or experts.

Experts tend to gravitate around a small set of products that work well for them. Beginners use few products in the first place.

Developing for beginners.

When you develop for beginners, you have to overcompensate by labeling most form elements, adding confirmation prompts, and offering a comprehensive help system. But these features don't make products simple.

There are ways to teach beginners such that they become intermediates after enough use. Documentation is one way. Brief instructions on how to get a product up and running, with descriptions of basic tasks, can guide beginners through a setup process. Another way is a prompt that appears on a product's first launch which explains certain elements or walks beginners through basic steps. None of these methods slow down users of other experience levels.

According to Alan Cooper, *About Face* (Wiley), 42, these three experience levels form a bell curve with intermediates at the hump:

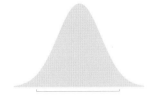

Developing for experts.

When you develop for experts, on the other hand, almost nothing needs to be documented, and the interface can be organized in any way that makes a shred of sense to you. You know that experts will tolerate it, that they'll be able to work with any level of complexity - but obviously developing for experts alienates beginners and intimidates intermediates. Targeting experts requires minimal empathy.

Developing for intermediates.

Targeting intermediates assumes that people are capable of picking up a device, understanding it after a short period of time, and that they don't need their hands held at every step. Intermediates have some knowledge of technological environments, but don't operate within them as if they were a fluently spoken second language. Products designed for this segment

Alan Cooper, *About Face* (Wiley), 249:

If we want users to like our products, we should design them to behave in the same manner as a likable person.

can be simple enough for most laypersons and powerful enough for most experts.

Most people are smart enough to figure things out, but many still need encouragement and support. Finding some common ground between the extremes of experience results in something that can be useful for everyone.

1.8. *Satisfy as many people as possible, and stop there.*

Our desires and preconceptions vary infinitely, and there's no way to make something that satisfies everyone. While this sounds like a major issue, it's easy to overcomplicate: running focus groups or market research to keep on top of things, or building too-complex products with features that appease vocal minorities.

Imagine you're running a store. Some customers buy things, and a handful return what they bought. If the latter didn't want what you offered, it doesn't reflect poorly on you.

Conversely, other customers decided to buy something because of how it looks at the time of their purchase, not how it might change in the future. As this applies to your product, every modification in every version risks alienating the customers that are likely to be your most ardent supporters. It's okay to say no to feature requests – even ones that appear common – if you think they'll detract from others' experiences.

Ultimately, you have to offer something great if anyone is going to stop by your store. You have to operate with the faith that customers will select the products that fit them best. The world has worked like this for hundreds of years, and those who work in our field shouldn't expect otherwise.

1.10 has more on giving great service and retaining business.

Obviously, you need to listen to users, or you'll build a bad reputation for yourself. But you still have to adhere to your own principles. What are the best ways to find balance here?

1.9. *Constraints are inherent to design.*

All good designs meet limitations, especially in their beginnings. While frustrating in the moment, constraint is one of the most useful things in design. Constraints are the walls that determine the product's shape, guide its character and spirit, and strengthen it in the process.

For more on iterating a product carefully, see 5.3.

Constraints also force you to develop faster. Developing faster benefits the product, because flaws are swiftly exposed and addressed, and features can be developed earlier.

1.10. Make a great impression before any sale.

Consider the perspective of someone that isn't an expert in technology, who doesn't keep up with its current trends. He's standing in a store, trying to pick out a printer. Here are the names of the products that he can choose from: E260DN, NX515, H470, MP620, C309A, J6480, MX700, P2055DN, HL-2040. While these printers are from different manufacturers, their model numbers are inscrutable, and it's impossible to associate manufacturer to model number.

These are the model numbers of real printers, out today. Never mind that MX700 is also the name of a computer mouse.

Our notional user has only each model's price, features, and *maybe* his friends' recommendation. If he has the latter, "get the P2055DN" sounds ridiculous (try saying it out loud!), and the model number is impossible to remember – and it may not even be the kind of printer that he's looking for.

Nothing about these printers is unique or special. But our user wants to make one part of his own life, and he's stuck in a fluorescent-lit Brutalist warehouse of a computer store looking at a bunch of undifferentiated cardboard boxes. In six months, the NX516 will come out, and nobody but the manufacturer will care. As a result, our user ends up purchasing something that appears to be crafted with little care for how he thinks and acts.

Our user may be in a brick-and-mortar store, but the same ideas apply to e-commerce.

If you go into a furniture store, it's obvious what the furniture does. The names of each product – chair, ottoman, sofa – imply what they do. People are around to help, when you have questions. Figuring the whole thing out is much simpler than buying a new computer or camera. So why is the computer store any different?

A product isn't just its physical device or its software. All parameters of a user's experience must be analyzed and addressed – and the most important place to do this is in the first impression. The first impression presents a wide range of considerations, from the packaging to the setup to the initial state.

Brand products well, to differentiate them, so they seem like something more than just a printer or camera or music player. Give them names that people can pronounce. Make good packaging. Make setup effortless and fun. A product isn't done until each of these aspects receive the same amount of care.

1.10.1. The product's marketing should reflect its quality.

Like the inscrutable printer model numbers above, marketing risks being too technical and inhumane. And given how marketing is usually people's first impression, it's surprising how frequently the pitch is disconnected from the product.

Marketing should clearly communicate the product's utility and mission. Understanding the symbolism behind a logo and product name aids both you and customers. It reminds you of your original mission and helps you to create an appropriate product. It's easier for customers to understand and remember.

Marketing shouldn't promise a specific lifestyle. Showing a bunch of nubile coeds in a convertible barreling down a street doesn't tell people anything about technology. Showing a product for a half-second at the end of a commercial doesn't tell anybody anything about it. Employing a viral hype scheme with a slow reveal tells people a story that is ultimately divorced from any actual experience with the product. Focus on the product itself. Show somebody using it: going through the prompts, hitting OK when a dialog box pops up. Show its utility.

Marketing shouldn't exaggerate performance. Instantaneous transitions between steps that realistically require more time promotes inaccurate expectations. A product should be advertised honestly. If you're unsatisfied with the product's performance when it's filmed for a commercial, then your users probably will be, too. Fix it.

Marketing shouldn't overstay its welcome. Once you've made the sale, get out of the user's and product's way.

1.10.2. *The product's setup process should exemplify its quality.*

A setup process should be as fast, simple, unambiguous, and effortless as possible. In the case of software, many operating systems offer default installation frameworks. Use them when they're available: don't waste time making an installer that users need to learn.

The setup process shouldn't obstruct other tasks, forcing unrelated applications to quit, or taking up such a substantial resource footprint that it renders the system unusable.

Products should be installed in a maximum of five steps:

1. open the setup program or turn the product on,
2. confirm the intent to install,
3. confirm the install location,
4. authorize with an administrator password, and
5. confirm a complete installation.

This is just one example of product setup, and only the first step is mandatory. For example, setting up new hardware should involve nothing more than plugging in a couple of cables and pressing the power button.

For many products, it's possible to eliminate one or more of these steps.

Streamline the process for more complex products by encouraging default installation procedures. This reduces the number of necessary steps, and keeps you focused on your product's most common configuration. Customization should be optional and set up as a quasimode.

For more on quasimodes, check out section 6.5.4.

1.10.3. The product's packaging should exemplify its quality.

Ideally, a product's packaging should reflect the product as an extension of its own design. But regardless of how appropriate the packaging is, it should be humane and unobtrusive.

For example, vacuum-sealed clamshell and side blister packaging are far more difficult to open than many alternatives. There is no reason why someone should have to take a sharp knife to a product's packaging. Nobody should have to expend significant effort to open a box. The problem is even worse for the young, the old, and the disabled. Standard cardboard boxes and snap-shut clamshells (without the sides welded together) are better options at reasonable cost.

Forcing users to destroy packaging also removes its potential for reuse if people return the product. Packaging should permit reuse by both the retailer and the user.

1.10.4. The product's manual should exemplify its quality.

When most people buy something new, they want to use it as quickly as possible. Many products come with quick start guides that help users get up and running quickly, while others ship with a 400 page tome of a user manual.

If a product is intended to be simple and consumer-friendly, the quick start guide should be all the manual that people need to operate it. Nobody has the time to read an enormous manual, which is a waste of paper and an intimidating deterrent.

1.10.5. The product's initial state should invite the user to interact with it.

Good products invite you to play with them. They promote the impression that using them is joyous and easy. This impression is often formed at the first screen that the user sees: the **initial state**, a blank, untouched slate with no data entered or behavior triggered.

The initial state conveys the product's slang, implying what to do with it. Here, users make snap judgments about how trustworthy and useful a product is. They'll try to figure out what kind of tool it is. What can it do? What is it supposed to do?

For more on how to predict next steps, see 6.1.2.

Then they'll try to work with it, triggering behavior on elements like buttons or text fields. How the product responds to those first stimuli implies its future behavior.

What does that blank slate look like? What does a user see as they try to orient themselves to the slang of something new? In what form does that invitation come?

Invitations can be *explicit*, accomplished with unambiguous copy that guides the user through opening steps. Or they can be *implicit*, accomplished by highlighting various elements – like an arrow pointing to a larger-than-usual text field. In either case, your first impression should prompt a specific action from the user.

For example, the goal on an e-commerce site is to convince someone to buy a product, so getting products into a shopping cart is an important step. Explicit cues can then guide users to interesting deals or new products.

Or consider a registration form with many required fields. Highlighting any required fields implicitly draws attention to them, while a progress indicator explicitly comforts the user in a form spanning multiple pages.

What's your product's first impression? Is it constructive? Is it kind? What does it ask people to do?

1.11. *Provide great service.*

Blogger Diana Kimball, on how she interacts with people:

Diana Kimball, "Trying," dianakimball.com, http://www.dianakimball.com/2008/09/trying.html

But still, I do my best to set the tone of every interaction at "extremely considerate." I try to do this even when the initial tone has been set at "less considerate," either by the other person or – more often – by circumstance. It is amazing how often the other person will respond in kind. You can actually live in a slightly more pleasant world by doggedly attempting to be considerate with everyone you meet. By not unnecessarily impinging on their time; by thanking them when you're grateful, apologizing when you're sorry, and smiling if the mood strikes you.

Service is the way that you treat any past, present, and future customers. Good service isn't about making sure nobody sues or slanders you. It's about making friends who tell others what you stand for. It's about making people happy.

Good service is about fixing problems for its own sake. Something, at some point, is going to dissatisfy one of your customers. Someone, at some point, will hesitate to buy into what you stand for. In every situation, good service helps you cement relationships and humanize your business. It extends the experience beyond the simple transaction of money for goods. And it's the best way to make users into fans.

If your work involves interacting with people at any point, you should serve them in the best way possible. Good service has to be honestly fought for. Nobody wins fans by cheating: favor comes naturally from making a good product and genuinely caring about people.

Service is a culture. No matter what, if you practice it, define it, and train employees to do the same, then service can permeate your organization and affect everyone's perception of you. You have to make it so that service is easy, encouraged, and rewarded. The shape of this depends on what your organization does; what matters is that it exists in the first place.

A great book about customer service is from outside our industry, and much of this section owes a debt to it. Check out Ari Weinzweig, *Zingerman's Guide to Giving Great Service* (Hyperion) if you want to find out how service was promoted in one small business.

1.11.1. *Define, measure, and reward good service.*

There's no way to provide good service if you don't define what it means for your company, there's no way to determine whether you're providing good service if you don't measure it, and there's no way to sustain a culture of good service if you don't reward your colleagues for providing it.

DEFINING SERVICE.

Service must be defined. Figure out specifically what you do to satisfy customers. You can establish service generally in a mission statement, but mission statements are empty promises without a practical plan to back them up.

Good things to integrate into a service plan include:

· Figuring out what's wrong promptly.
· Apologizing for any problems that arose.
· Fixing issues unquestioningly.
· Going out of your way to make sure customers are happy.

MEASURING SERVICE.

Service can be measured in many ways. What you choose to measure depends on what kinds of service you want to provide.
Some good starting points include:

· Calling customers back to ask them about their experiences.
· Sending out surveys.
· Recording all complaints to determine the biggest problems.

- Recording all compliments and trying to figure out which parts of your business are succeeding or failing.
- Tracking and timing the turnaround of support queries.
- Figuring out patterns: who places repeat orders of a specific product, who comes back for a wide array of products, who places more support requests than usual, or who refers others to your business the most.

REWARDING SERVICE.

Develop incentives and prizes. Make them part of your daily, weekly, or monthly routine. When applicable, tie employees' bonuses to the quality of service that they provide. If you make sure that service is measurable, you'll be able to figure out who's providing it well, and you'll be able to cite exceptional instances.

1.11.2. *Underpromise and overdeliver.*

Managing users' expectations is a big part of giving great service. But when you're dedicated to making people happy, you have to fight the temptation to promise them things that may be impossible to fulfill.

If you underpromise, though, you set expectations that you can meet or exceed. Underpromised goals are grounded in what you're already good at doing. Set deadlines too far, financial projections too low, feature sets too thin, and product launches too modest. If you keep your estimates reasonable, customers have no reason to believe otherwise. And when you overdeliver, customers feel special because you're going above and beyond what they expected.

1.11.3. *Take responsibility for your mistakes.*

It's painful to admit when we've screwed up, but at some point we all have to do it. On the bright side, fixing problems gracefully often fosters more trust than when nothing goes wrong in the first place.

Don't be afraid to take the blame when things go wrong, even when you don't think the problems are your fault. Part of good service involves wanting to understand why the customer is upset, and doing whatever you can to fulfill their needs. Address problems quickly and take immediate, forthright, unflinching responsibility for them.

1.11.4. *Encourage feedback.*

You don't need someone on call 24/7, but you should provide a way for users to submit questions and comments. Ensure that there are open, but unobtrusive, feedback channels.

On a website, a feedback mechanism can be placed on every page. In an application, feedback can reside in a contextual menu item. On mobile devices, a feedback link can be placed in the application's preferences.

1.11.5. *Don't systematize your conversation.*

Architect Christopher Alexander, on first impressions:

Have you ever walked into a public building and been processed by the receptionist as if you were a package?

This should be asked about your service, which can't afford to treat frustrated users as machines.

Don't route phone calls through a labyrinthine system where users must diagnose their own problems. It's up to *you* to figure out what's wrong. Send queries to real humans, who can determine the problem much faster and more accurately than users can, and handle it accordingly. Support staff should work without quotas or time limits.

You may object that this doesn't make economic sense. And while it may not be financially justifiable, that isn't the point of making users happy. Though there's potential financial loss involved with hiring extra support staff, or providing free products or services in apology, the word-of-mouth benefits and repeat business more than make up for it. The intangibles matter.

If you establish a reputation for good service, customers will be much happier to give you their business again and again – and it feels good to know that you've done the right thing.

1.11.6. *Answer questions quickly.*

Answering questions quickly shows that your company is concerned about the well-being of its customers beyond the sale, which will translate – if intangibly – to strong word-of-mouth promotion and future business.

Beyond that, though, people simply don't want their time wasted. Questions submitted electronically should be replied to in under 36 hours. Phone calls shouldn't take more than an hour, except when seriously dire troubleshooting is necessary.

Christopher Alexander, *A Pattern Language* (Oxford University Press), 705.

While not directly related to software, Christopher Alexander has influenced software development theories considerably, and is returned to frequently in this book. Section 2.6 applies his idea of modular patterns to interaction design. His books *A Pattern Language*, *The Timeless Way of Building*, and *Notes on the Synthesis of Form* (Oxford University Press) are pretty fast reads despite their length; and while they concern architecture and city planning, they remain tremendously inspiring.

Unanswered questions should be prioritized based on how long they've waited in the queue.

And even if your answer is "I don't know," explaining *why* you don't know, and doing it promptly, can help comfort users. It implies your interest in solving their problems, and it opens the door for future support calls or second opinions from other team members.

1.11.7. Establish a case thread for each problem, and archive cases for each customer.

Even though you should enact your own system of service – a way to file issues and collect data on recurring trends – you don't want to appear too rigorous to the customer. Having an unstructured support *front end*, where customers aren't routed through a maze of questions, means your support staff is personally responsible for organizing their concerns.

Every new issue should be the beginning of a **case thread**, and each customer contact should correspond to a separate post in a given case thread until the issue is confirmedly resolved.

Threads have a one-to-one correspondence with customers' problems. They should be updated every time you contact the customer, or the customer contacts you back, about a given problem. Threads help track frequently occurring types of problems, and the steps taken to solve them.

All of a customer's threads comprise his or her **case history**. The customer's case history should be consulted at the beginning of every contact, to better understand the context of their problem and what progress has been made.

Customers never see this infrastructure, of course. Case threads and histories are for your own benefit: they help prioritize repeated problems, and they isolate customers who are having significant trouble.

1.11.8. Link threads to staff members.

Likewise, each case thread should be associated with a support team member. Staff members should own whatever threads they initiate, because the first contact with a customer will yield most of the significant information. Moreover, users are comforted by establishing a relationship with a specific person; and your staff will be more invested in solving complex problems, rather than diverting them around the organization.

1.11.9. Treat your colleagues as well as your customers.

Coworkers should treat each other as well as their customers; even if they may not be best friends outside work, they should put those differences aside in the workplace. Internal issues should be addressed with just as much respect and sensitivity as customer complaints.

It's easy for this to come off as some lofty, unrealistic manifesto for world peace. But if you start with this perspective, it's easier to come up with practical solutions for mediating differences and treating each other well. If you truly walk the walk of good service, it takes less effort to reapply your rules to internal affairs.

1.12. Don't let popular opinion dictate the interface if it conflicts with your mission.

Targeting on a specific group of users – a restricted demographic, or specialists in a field – will result in a more focused product. Design decisions are then made with someone specific in mind, rather than trying to please everyone. It also ensures a stronger customer base to weather competition, and they won't rise in revolt at your slightest misstep.

Know when and how to say no. You can decline requests for additional features if they conflict with your beliefs or don't reflect the product's mission. If your business isn't perfect for each and every customer, somebody else's may be.

One thing on your side is users' need for specialized products. Consider the countless photo editing programs with varyingly complex feature sets. Some users just want to crop and change an image's white balance; others require more complicated functionality like layering and masking. Both sets of requirements are valid, but they mandate a need for separate products. Targeting a specific skill set or demographic helps focus your product and whittle away anything unnecessary.

1.13. Stay small and autonomous.

Small teams emphasize the individual. We work better and happier when we connect with others, and connecting is much easier to do in a small team. When our efforts show demonstrable progress, we feel empowered to make a difference.

There's an increasing trend among design firms to be small and independent. Many more designers are finding success as freelancers. Even within large companies, managers are

The different ways to encourage workplace cooperation are as variant as company cultures. One example is hashed out at Michael Lopp, "B.A.B.," Rands in Repose, http://randsinrepose.com/archives/2010/03/19/bab.html .

organizing their workers into small teams, so that their companies can *feel* small. As you grow, ensure that small teams are preserved as well as possible.

1.14. *Create products in the name of utility first, progress second, and money third.*

It's essential to find ways to make money, of course, but that should always be a secondary motivation to making something useful. Products should be useful above all else. Resist the temptation to alter the product, even if the changes promise to make you more money, whenever those changes would compromise its utility.

It's tempting, but wrong, to taint the goal of utility with other objectives. Your integrity is tied to your product's integrity.

1.15. *The more successful your product becomes, the greater the need for humility and simplicity.*

Ideally, your product is wildly successful, with sales beyond your expectations and stratospheric consumer trust. Suddenly, many constraints disappear: you're able to upgrade to a larger office, hire more employees, and have more resources. The risk of losing the humility that paved your way to greatness suddenly pervades your life. Caving to the temptation threatens the intangible character that made your product successful, along with the incentive to prove yourself.

Humility is not as obvious or measurable as a good interface. It's ethereal, ambiguous, created from mindset and behavior. And the only diagnostic you can run on it is your own capacity for reflection.

Many things change as an organization grows, but humility shouldn't be one of them. It should be a core principle that governs all of your dealings. Out of it comes trust in your colleagues and the incentive to keep doing great things.

Simplicity resists scaling. As your product becomes more successful, the incentive to add features and please more people becomes ever greater. The need to preserve simplicity becomes more pressing because the resistance increases from increasingly many fronts, in ever greater magnitude. It takes effort to protect simplicity, but it will be repaid with an iconic, timeless product. Does it feel whole? What's missing from it? What can be taken away? What can be modified? How would it look and behave *then*?

The **character** of an interface is the way that it talks to you, as well as the way that it allows you to talk with it. It should be consistent and unified in all parts: speaking with one voice, and learning in one language.

Consistency aids clarity to every part of the product.

2.1. Apply a consistent layout with consistent negative space.

We have to start building somewhere. All products begin with a blank canvas: no text, no buttons, no graphics. An **element** is anything that alters a blank canvas. Buttons, switches, speakers, headphone jacks, keyboards, scroll wheels, scroll bars, paragraphs of text, labels, input fields, icons, graphics, title bars, drop-down menus, borders, and individual pixels are some elements that we encounter in modern technology, and we haven't begun to exhaust the iterations of their forms. **Controls** are elements that, when prompted by the user, trigger behavior.

Layout is how elements and groups of elements are arranged with respect to one another. When users begin to interact with a product, they immediately establish familiarity with the locations of various elements. Shifting elements around from page to page, or prompt to prompt, forces users to expend unwanted effort on finding each element again, which erodes their trust. Because of this, layout should be as consistent as possible.

Jan Tschichold defines layout as a hierarchy, which makes sense in graphic design as well:

Every part of a text relates to every other part by a definite, logical relationship of emphasis and value, predetermined by content.

Meanwhile, Paul Rand values the subtle relationships between the elements of an interface (or poster, book, advertisement, etc.):

To believe that a good layout is produced merely by making a pleasing arrangement of some visual miscellany (photos, type, illustrations) is an erroneous conception of the graphic designer's function. What is implied is that a problem can be solved simply by pushing things around until something happens.

In interaction design, we face the same issues: grouping, context, meaning. Excess frill or semantic ambiguity can send mixed messages. Finally, Kenya Hara hits on the goal:

A designer creates an architecture of information within the mind of the recipient of his work.

2:

Consistency
& Character

Jan Tschichold, *The New Typography* (University of California Press), 67.

Paul Rand, *A Designer's Art* (Yale University Press), 4.

Kenya Hara, *Designing Design* (Lars Müller Publishers), 156.

One example of a modular scale is the Fibonacci Sequence, where each term is the sum of the two preceding terms: 1,2, 3, 5, 8, 13, 21, 34, and so on into infinity. The ratio of the nth term to the n-1th term (so $^{34}/_{21}$, for example) approaches the golden section φ, or approximately 1.618, as n approaches infinity.

Robert Bringhurst, *The Elements of Typographic Style* (Hartley & Marks Publishers) and Le Corbusier, *Le Modulor* (Birkhäuser Basel) discuss modular scales at greater length.

Jan Tschichold, in 1930, from eye magazine, "Faith in asymmetry," Eye Review, http://www.eyemagazine.com/review.php?id=151&rid=718&set=780: "White space is to be regarded as an active element, not a passive background." Even today, it's worth considering negative space as an element unto itself.

6.3.3 discusses how to use grid systems and typographic baselines to enforce more elegant layouts.

If two elements exist at the same time, they automatically exist in a relationship with each other. When you add a third element, each element interacts with one another, producing six distinct relationships. The complexity of this becomes daunting on paper, but we have the ability to differentiate between, and draw relationships among, many elements at once.

To complicate the matter further, the negative space between elements matters as well. Margins should express an internal language that implies the location and significance of each grouping, without creating undue tension. Layout organizes both the existence *and absence* of elements.

Best practices in organizing layout have existed in print design for centuries, thanks in part to the development of **modular scales**, which are mathematically constructed systems of proportions that determine the relative measurements on a page. The units of a modular scale are indivisible, and not of a consistent multiple. Bookmakers use modular scales to compose the margins of books such that they develop proportion, balance, heft, and tension. If it's worked for them for so long, why not apply that principle to an interface's layout?

Whether you're setting text, graphical buttons, or forms, the principles behind the arrangement of content are no different. These days, designers and typographers can place text blocks and titles on their canvases near-instantaneously, without any thought that their actions may have implied meaning – but doing so produces a careless product.

Fortunately, modern trends promote more sensitive considerations of white space in layout. Many designers in both print and interactive media advocate modular scales and typographic baselines to give text blocks rhythm. These help you create interfaces with more visual balance.

Let's imagine you're trying to develop an application that views any sort of published content on the web. This could include blog posts, images, video, or status updates. The application probably offers different views of that data: perhaps posts that mention the user or link back to her website, or updates from a specific feed or person, or a group of feeds. Or, if you're viewing an image gallery, the listing could correspond to a specific event, instead of a chronological sort.

These are all sensible ways that people want to view data. And more likely than not, that data will be readable if it's displayed consistently from view to view. The title of a post, the post itself, the date that it was published, the page title, navigation, and so on should all appear in the same locations. And while the data types vary, each type should be laid out and sorted in a consistent way.

Consistency trains users to expect the position and appearance of every element in a layout. When a layout is consistent, it's easier for them to learn *how* to learn what you want to show, and to develop a lasting bond with your product.

2.2. *Apply consistent behavior.*

As mentioned in 1.6, a product's behavior is the way that it responds to user input. Combine elements with their corresponding behaviors, and you have a complete product.

Inconsistent behavior is a highly visible problem for the same reasons as inconsistent layout. But sometimes the solutions aren't readily apparent, or they take too much effort to build consistently, or it's difficult to change the attitudes of the product's developers.

The basics of behavior can be defined rigorously.

Paths.

Users conduct a series of discrete **steps** to accomplish any task: pressing a button, navigating between form fields, entering data, etc. In succession, these steps comprise a **path** to complete the task. Multiple paths comprise one entire **interaction**, or a relationship between a user and a product, from the time when it is picked up (or opened) to when it is put down (or closed). Finally, a user's **experience** is the sum of all of their interactions.

The branches of a product's paths can become very complicated, attaining a recursive, fractal complexity. If there are many ways to begin an interaction, then you automatically have to support, and account for, those many different use cases. And as use cases branch out, you may have to account for many *common* paths. It makes sense to simplify the number of paths as much as possible, so the product is easy for users to learn, and for you to maintain.

Monotony.

When different paths are required to accomplish the same task, they should behave identically. The best way to ensure consistency between similar paths is to pare them down as much as possible – ideally to only one. An interface is **monotonous** if it has a one-to-one mapping between paths and desired tasks.

I call these *paths*, which may seem novel, but the idea has been in interaction design for a little while now. Alan Cooper calls the same thing *command vectors*, defined as "distinct techniques for allowing users to issue instructions to [a] program": Alan Cooper, *About Face* (Wiley), 551.

I use the term *path* because I think it's a nicer way to visualize the user trying to get to the destination of a completed task. If you read other books and see *command vector*, they're talking about the same thing.

Your keyboard's "caps lock" key is the most classic example of turning a mode on and off.

Jef Raskin, *The Humane Interface* (Addison-Wesley Professional), 67.

For more on the constraints afforded by a product's context, see 2.8.

Monotony has a strong connection to **modes**, which are defined as any kind of setting that a user can trigger to activate a different set of behaviors on an otherwise identical interface. Jef Raskin, who coined the term "monotonous," elaborates:

Monotony is the dual of modelessness in an interface. In a modeless interface, a given user gesture has one and only one result: Gesture **g** *always results in action* **a**. *However, there is nothing to prevent a second gesture,* **h**, *from also resulting in action* **a**.

The past few years of technology have favored monotony, but the prevailing trend has been against it. Designers and developers assume that users want freedom in their choice of path, so they provide an overwhelmingly broad array of ways to arrive there, with customizing functions providing still more. While one can argue that lowering the number of paths to just one is constricting, the point is a fallacy if that particular path is obvious and learnable. It falls on the designer's shoulders to make paths easy to use in the first place. *Fundamental tasks should always be monotonous; that is, they should have a one-to-one mapping to paths.*

Monotony is often hard to implement because of functional constraints, the elements' context, and the desires of other team members – but if elements are conveyed with as little behavioral ambiguity as possible, then monotony is indeed feasible.

Before you can design a monotonous interaction, you have to have faith that people will try to learn your product. It's a lot easier to have that faith if you make the product simple. So it's a self-fulfilling cycle: making the product simpler gives you the confidence that users will understand it more easily, which in turn gives you the confidence that making it simpler was the right choice in the first place. You have to have the right momentum to reach this conclusion, and it's just as easy to take the opposite road, towards embracing complexity.

Editing down existing interfaces to be monotonous is a crucial but difficult task. Sometimes it requires resolving conflicting desires between colleagues: one wants the product to accomplish a task in X way, and another wants the task to be accomplished through Y, so they assume it's okay to compromise by using both methods, that both are somehow right. Two of the hardest parts of interaction design are recognizing that this line of thinking doesn't scale to more complex products, and having the courage to say no to these additional paths. Consensus decisions lead to less clarity in vision than taking the initiative to say that *this* is the way things should be, offering research and testing as proof, presenting a grounded and practical solution, and expecting the rest of the team to trust that you aren't screwing things up. Trust is a big part of what makes monotony so difficult.

AN EXAMPLE.

Let's take a look at a word processor and figure out some ways to cut down the number of steps and paths that it requires. The first thing to do is create a new document. The operating system has a FILE menu, so we focus to it with our mouse and click. Then there's a NEW option. One more focus. A submenu then opens with the options DOCUMENT... and DOCUMENT FROM TEMPLATE... Select DOCUMENT... and a modal dialog prompts us to specify the parameters of our file: page size, margins, and whether you have facing pages.

All of these are reasonable things that we might want to modify, but they can also be changed after we've created the document, with a preference pane. We decide to change none of them, and hit OK to create the document. That makes four steps: clicking FILE, then NEW, then DOCUMENT..., then OK. And while there's a keyboard shortcut that reduces the number of steps to two (it still pops up the modal dialog), this is the minimum number that it takes to create a new document without knowing the shortcut.

Eliminating the dialog is an immediate and obvious way to shorten the path by one more step. At this point, we have a few options, depending on what trade-offs we're willing to make.

5.9 discusses preferences in depth.

1. We can make both NEW DOCUMENT and NEW DOCUMENT FROM TEMPLATE primary menu items, which would increase the length of the primary menu but keep the user from having to hover over to a submenu.
2. If the program has a toolbar for frequently-used functions, one of the two NEW options can correspond to an icon on the default configuration for that toolbar.
3. On opening the application, a (hopefully non-modal) dialog could pop up that prompts the user to either create a new document or open an existing document. The new dialog may even teach the user the keyboard shortcut to create a new file: "To create a new document in the future, hit command-N."

These are just three options, and more than one can be built. All of them reduce the number of steps to two or one - a 50% or 75% improvement - and they do so in a way that doesn't sacrifice the program's functionality.

This isn't some situation that I fabricated to prove the magic of this process. This is how you create a new document in the software that I'm using to typeset this book. It's a finished product used by thousands of people, on version number 6.0. And there's still considerable room for improvement, so that users remain in the flow of their original tasks, facing as few distractions as possible.

And in this case, it's just one feature of dozens that could be improved this way. It's a question of sensitive editing: of cutting out what doesn't *need* to be there. We do this with our own writing all the time, shortening it for clarity and impact. Why not do the same with technology?

LANGUAGE.

Interfaces can be read for underlying meaning. As users interact with a product, they discover, and subconsciously process, creators' intent.

Language means more than just well-written copy. Products have their own verbal, visual, and behavioral languages. **Language**, as applied here, is the communication of any stimulus – whether visual, auditory, or otherwise.

A product should have a consistent visual language. Functionally similar prompts, output, and elements should appear in the same places, displayed in the same ways, with the same character to them. Conversely, separate paths and separate functions should be distinguished.

A product should have a consistent behavioral language. Any elements that behave the same should look the same, and any elements that behave differently should look different. Functions that do not pertain to the task at hand should be disabled or invisible, and their disabled state should be immediately evident. Pliant elements should look different from unpliant elements.

This is often referred to as a "ghosted" button or menu item, made lighter than the other options to imply that it isn't clickable For example:

pliant unpliant

SOME EXAMPLES OF INCONSISTENT BEHAVIORAL LANGUAGE.

- *Similar behavior but different appearance.* A proprietary content management system has multiple ways to create new content: either through a green + link in the upper-right of most pages' main content areas, a much larger (and more three-dimensional) + icon in a tab above the content area, or a text drop-down list that outlines many common functions, including an option to add new content. This leads users into believing that each way of creating new content could be slightly different, or that there isn't any way to create new data on a page lacking one of the three functions.

The best way to solve a problem like this is to keep the smaller green text link in the same place, on *every* page where content can be added, and to eliminate all instances of the other two designs. It takes up less space, is functionally unambiguous, isn't image-based, and doesn't require translation between languages. The function of the + would correspond to the type of data that's being viewed or edited at the time.

- *Similar appearance but different behavior.* Based on the appearance of elements, users form expectations about their behavior. If an element works differently, it should look different.
- *Unambiguous pliancy.* Rather than pop up an error message on controls that someone isn't supposed to access at a given time, make the element in question unpliant.

2.3. *The words in an interface are part of the interface.*

Design extends to copy, from advertising to branding to the product itself. Copy is part of the interface, and every word is a design decision. Words are used in form labels, page titles, menu names, controls, dialog prompts, and product names. The user experiences this as much as underlying functionality, and it should be as straightforward and elegant as the other parts of the product.

2.3.1. *Adopt a kind tone and a hopeful tenor.*

Tone can't be faked; it's a clear indicator of the product's character. Words should be as kind and humane as the product is. They should promote a sense of hope to the user, that the product is capable of filling their need.

2.3.2. *Copy should be descriptive.*

Copy should elucidate the function of an interface, rather than describing how great the product is. Words should be edited in favor of practicality, each word relevant to the user's goals.

2.3.3. *Copy should be non-technical.*

Technical error messages, with meaningless numbers or stack traces, are condescending. Messages should be sensible, natural, and written in complete sentences when appropriate.

A **stack trace** is a report of the active parts of a given computer program, frequently used for debugging.

2.3.4. Write real words.

In the past couple of years, the profession of content strategist has formed to fill the blank slates created by information architects and interface designers. So much copy, especially copy written for the web, urgently needs to be cleaned up by people dedicated to the task of creating and editing the product's mission and vision. Copy is not an afterthought: it's the first thing people look to when they try to understand what *any* product is about.

Writing "lorem ipsum" or "copy goes here" text may make for a nice-looking wireframe, but it doesn't impart any sort of utility. It's also lazy: it takes less time to copy and paste from a block of lorem ipsum than it does to think about writing real content.

Real content helps you envision the product's real-world use.

2.3.5. Write in either the plural first or second person.

I generally prefer the plural first person, but depending on the situation, you may need to use the second person.

Make sure you use the right personal pronoun, and try to use it consistently throughout. First person involves "I." Plural first person (also called "grammatical person") involves "we." Second person involves "you."

Consider some sample feedback messages, written in different tenses. In each case, one of these messages sounds less awkward than the other two, and the singular first person sounds like the product is anthropomorphized.

- First person: "I will help you create a new document."
- Plural first person: "We'll create a new document."
- Second person: "You will create a new document."

I would use the plural first person here, because the second person is too accusatory.

- First person: "I didn't understand your input."
- Plural first person: "We didn't understand your input."
- Second person: "You didn't enter a recognized command."

- First person: "I sent your message."
- Plural first person: "The message was sent."
- Second person: "You sent your message."

- First person: "I couldn't find any updates for the applications in your library."
- Plural first person: "We couldn't find any updates for the applications in your library."

However, the second person works better here.

- Second person: "There are no updates for any of the applications in your library."

2.3.6. Apply consistent copy.

Make sure every word in the product is vetted for consistency, and make sure that developers are provided with guidance for writing labels and feedback.

Consistent labels.

Form labels should be consistent. If two different forms ask for an address, one should not read "Address" and the other "Home Address."

- Use either OK or SUBMIT, not both.
- Use either CANCEL or START OVER, not both.
- POST, SEND, SUBMIT, and SAVE all connote different actions.
- Depending on which country was entered, a lookup procedure could be used to set to the right nomenclature, from POSTAL CODE to ZIP CODE; as well as among STATE, PROVINCE, and Territory. Use POSTAL CODE if you can't change this term dynamically.

CANCEL is more familiar than START OVER.

Consistent feedback.

Feedback should always read with similar syntax and structure. If you're formatting one message in a particular way, it stands to reason that every other message should, when possible, read similarly.

For instance, if you write ARE YOU SURE? in one confirmation prompt, then you should not write CONFIRM: Y/N in another.

Feedback involves behavior as well. For example, if you're deleting a row from a table, one delete function shouldn't fade the row out while another slides the row out of view. Each of these functions should do one or the other.

Consistent errors.

Error messages should be formatted clearly and consistently. Here's a set of real error messages, quoted from finished products and stripped of obvious identifiers, that show room for improvement. We can reword these so they make more sense, don't condescend to the user, and offer an opportunity to provide feedback.

Error. The operation completed successfully.

Internally confused messages send the wrong impression. If the operation were indeed successful, the word "Error" has no place in the message.

The application [application name] quit unexpectedly. [The operating system] and other applications are not affected. Click Relaunch to launch the application again. Click Report to see more details or send a report to [the developer].

Error feedback after every crash is redundant. Usually, users either want to report errors whenever they occur, or don't want to report errors at all.

The application's preferences could provide users with a setting to deal with errors: for instance, to automatically send *all* error reports to the developer, which would remove the need for a prompt every time something goes wrong.

Ideally, though, such a setting could apply to all applications in the operating system, with a way for software developers to collect all error reports for their respective products.

In what way would such an option differ from what already exists, besides removing the continual intrusion?

Sorry, [application name] crashed unexpectedly. If you were not doing anything confidential (entering passwords or other private information), you can help to improve the application by reporting the problem.

What if the user *was* indeed doing something confidential? Is there a way to remove or obscure identifying information from the error report to protect the user's privacy? If sensitive information is absolutely necessary, is encryption a possible compromise?

If so, then the first clause and parenthetical explanation of that sentence could be removed. Strive to be concise; wordy responses waste the user's time.

Beta-only warning message – not to be localized: UMESSAGE *buffer full! Should never happen. Generate fewer messages.*

This error message appeared in a completed, post-beta product, but post-beta users have no need for it. If developers care about error output during beta, they should code a way to toggle verbose reporting in the source code, for when the product ships.

"Should never happen" is a sentence fragment that should be rewritten as a sentence.

Localization is a term solely used by, and relevant to, software engineers. A shipping product should generate error messages that are *only pertinent to users*, not developers.

Users have no idea what the term "UMESSAGE buffer" means – or why it matters. It should be defined or reworded, for example to: "An internal error has occurred. The message buffer is full."

An unhandled error occurred in the GUI, further errors may be reported. -6

Errors should never be referred to by their number, even when accompanying descriptions. Diagnostic numbers help developers, not users.

While you likely know what a GUI is, most people don't.

What does it mean for an error to be "unhandled?" At press time, the powers that be haven't admitted "unhandled" into any English dictionary.

Why is the sentence broken with a comma, rather than a period or semicolon?

Worst of all, why announce that further errors may be reported? It gives the user no assurance that the product works. If further errors are possible, is it time to force the program to restart?

A dialog box is open. Please close the dialog box before continuing.

Modal dialog boxes should be kept to an absolute minimum to begin with, and the need for a dialog box about a dialog box shouldn't exist in any application.

The message implies a recursion that makes no logical sense. Messages should follow the logic of the application, which the user should be able to figure out.

A system error has occurred. Please contact the support team.

This message doesn't describe the nature of the error, and the product doesn't automatically report it.

A colleague sent this error message to me. He's on the support team. When diagnosing his own software, he frequently encounters this message for a variety of problems. So who supports the support team?

[application name] did not shutdown tidily. Check /home/user/. appname/logs/save for diagnostic log files and consider reporting them to the [application name] team if this is the result of an application error. Also check the Wiki (see the Help menu) for "[application name] Disappears"

This message appears when you open a program after a system crash. It assumes that users have significant experience in system-level debugging and research. Few users will expend the effort that the message requests. Programs should recover gracefully after a force quit. Error messages of this type shouldn't exist, because they're unhelpful and misleading.

Why does the error message refer to a hidden path, requiring a special search on the command line?

What's a log file? What's the difference between diagnostic log files and other kinds of log files? Are they saved in different locations?

How can a user determine what kind of error constitutes an application error?

Consult the Wiki? While many users know what a wiki is, many more don't – and most won't care. Regardless, using the term "help wiki" clarifies its role.

Why and how does the application "disappear?"

Usage errors abound. What does it mean to shut down "tidily?" Why is "shutdown" one word? Why is the final sentence missing a period?

And again: why does the program lack a way to automatically report the error?

Catastrophic failure.

This was the entire message. Had I read this and not known better, I'd think a sinkhole was about to open underneath my computer and swallow it forever.

You should reboot a computer!!

This message appeared at the end of a program's installation.

Which computer? Any computer? Can I choose which one? What will that do? And why *two* exclamation points?

Why not simply: *Please restart your computer now.* Or better yet, does the operating system provide a native function that serves the same purpose?

Sweat the details in every error message. You may think that a misplaced semicolon or two exclamation points ultimately makes no difference in how people perceive your product. You may think that picking out a few absurdly bad error messages is too satirical for serious critique. But user complaints about poorly-written error messages abound – and in severe cases, you get something like "Catastrophic failure."

For an amusing take on the subject, see Ben Zimmer, "Crash Blossoms," The New York Times, http://www. nytimes.com/2010/01/31/ magazine/31FOB-onlanguage-t.html .

Detailed copy editing is important in any field where words exist to be read. Your customers will care about what you have to say to them. Meet them at least halfway.

CONSISTENT HELP.

Like everything else in your product, help should be consistent in its language, voice, and tone.

Information architects and content strategists help make the copy on websites consistent, readable, and navigable. Users expect the same of the web's help files and support documents: they should be easy to search, common problems should be prominently displayed, and their display should be consistent from entry to entry.

When developing software, your operating system will likely already have a system in place for help documents. Use it. Don't make it a placeholder for where to find the *real* help – put the actual information there, and format it in the right way.

2.3.7. Apply a consistent tone.

Nobody intentionally writes with inconsistent tone, but it can creep into products when they become large enough, as more than one person is charged with writing.

Even if you don't consider yourself a good writer, it's possible to train yourself to write good copy. All it takes is being sensitive to what your product says to people.

Tone is a matter of attitude. Writing, however, is a *craft* that is practiced – one learns to write like learning to play a musical instrument, or mastering a trade. Nobody is born a great writer, but countless dedicated people have *made* themselves into great writers.

Let's look at some copy that may unintentionally give the wrong impression. Syntax errors have been some of the most common types of errors in technology since the dawn of personal computing.

They take many forms, from the terse:
- *Syntax error.*
- *Inappropriate entry.*
- *Overflow*

to the verbose:
- *No standard web pages containing all your search terms were found. Your search – [entry] – did not match any documents.*

Suggestions: Make sure all words are spelled correctly. Try different keywords. Try more general keywords. Try fewer keywords.

to the technical:
- *Incorrect form: must be in form [entry].*
- *-bash: [entry]: command not found*
- *Not Found: The requested* URL *[entry] was not found on this server.*
- *[Application name] isn't sure what to do with your input.*

to the personified:
- *I'm sorry, I don't know what to do with that.*
- *No matches. Try being more specific.*

to the humorous:
- *Uh oh. Something very bad has happened. We're working on it.*
- *We couldn't find any results matching [entry]. We give up!*
- *This wave is experiencing some slight turbulence, and may explode. If you don't wanna explode, please re-open the wave. Some recent changes may not be saved.*

Independent of the content of these error messages, they imply different moods. Some are stoic and indifferent. Some are funny. Some are comforting. Some are useless. Some are needlessly verbose. Some don't even convey the right thing; the one where "something very bad has happened" came up when I typed gibberish into a search blank and hit enter. How is that very bad?

Each of them, however, reflects on whomever wrote it. When multiple people are working on a product, each runs the risk of inconsistent tone by subtly projecting his or her intentions onto the copy. This has to be accounted for, although it's a subtle problem to criticize well.

If you grouse about the connotations of a single word or phrase, you're viewed as splitting hairs, fighting battles over too-small details. But these things *do* matter, and they *are* worth fighting over. All successful products concern themselves with smoothing out the details of copy. As with all other parameters of your product, neglecting the copy is a big problem when your trustworthiness and reputation are at stake.

2.4. Apply consistent graphic design.

Because trends change over time, any specific rules about graphic design will be obsolete in short order. But no matter when you're designing, you're still building a consistent interface, not a Dadaist poster. All optical parameters should appear unified, balanced, and coherent. They should convey ideas with as much clarity as possible.

There are countless ways that graphic design can be inconsistent, but some common problems are easily solved:

- All icons should look like they're created by the same hand.
- Don't mix typefaces at random. Better yet, use as few typeface families as possible - ideally one serif and one sans.
- Text should have consistent letter spacing and leading.
- Use no more than three shades of the same hue for establishing a hierarchy.
- On websites, represent links in only one color.
- Favor the plain and familiar over the flashy, the preposterous, the absurd.

Discard this rule if you are, in fact, making a Dadaist poster. For more on color and graphics, see 3.4.

2.5. Don't create separate products with feature sets geared towards beginners or experts.

All users begin sometime, and at some point, *all* of your users use your product for the first time. Still, it's condescending and denigrating to assume that the user is a beginner. Establishing separate interfaces for different experience levels is needlessly complex, time-consuming, and counterproductive towards educating people.

Beginners tend to become intermediates quickly, because nobody invested in using a product wants to remain unaware of how it works. At the same time, though, few intermediates tend to become experts, because most people don't see the point in memorizing keyboard shortcuts or extensively customizing their tools. The vast majority of users are intermediates, and you should design with this group in mind.

There's one exception to this: any interface that people deliberately use for brief periods of time, like a kiosk or ATM. But the majority of products are designed for longer periods of use than these.

In short, this means two things. First, all the fancy customization options you're building into your preferences pane will be used by a tiny minority of people. Second, your default settings will be used by the overwhelming majority. Take the intermediate path and make sure that your application is learnable, by default, without the need for training wheels.

For more on targeting intermediates, see 1.7.

2.6. Reuse code, elements, and behaviors.

It may seem like a tall order to enforce consistency in every single aspect of the product, but fortunately there are many ways to encourage it. Modern software development favors consistency and reuse, from graphic design to code.

Systematic reuse isn't *essential*, but convenience, maintainability, and consistency depend on it. You made it once; why expend the effort to make it again? Why not design it right the first time? It's faster, easier, more elegant, and less expensive.

Software engineers embrace object-oriented programming (or oop), which applies reuse notions to code. Just as the Industrial Revolution gave us mechanical reproduction as an efficient way to improve our standards of living, object-oriented programming provides ways to make programming more efficient.

One pillar of object-oriented programming is the concept of a design pattern. The term "pattern" is coined in Christopher Alexander's books *The Timeless Way of Building* and *A Pattern Language* (Oxford University Press), which apply patterns to the design and construction of houses and towns in a modular, efficient, and humane way. While a series of patterns is the central tenet of both books, Alexander never formally defines the term, so I'll take a stab at it. A **pattern** is the definition of a recurring problem; the discussion of its essence and implications; and an abstracted, reusable, visually expressed design solution. A group of patterns interact with one another to create an entire system called a **pattern language**.

Elements are patterns of relationships that coalesce into working features. Place an element on a blank canvas and it alters the canvas; place *another* element there, and it alters *both the canvas and the other element*. The use of patterns is a good way to simplify, aggregate, and manage the relationships among elements, groups of elements, and their behavior. They help you to identify problems before they become too difficult to fix, and then they abstract those problems to give you better perspective for approaching future tasks.

How to create patterns.

If you ever repeatedly encounter a certain kind of problem and find yourself solving it in the same way, it may be time to use a pattern. There are many libraries of interaction design patterns, and creating patterns for yourself is easy as well. Establish a toolbox of commonly reused ideas – controls, processes, front end appearances – and consult it regularly.

An example.

Take a website that requires users to login. Historically, login has taken many forms. Login can exist for first-time users who'd

If you're interested in a good pattern language for interaction design, check out Jennifer Tidwell, *Designing Interfaces* (O'Reilly).

The relationships between elements is further discussed in 2.1.

have to create an account, or for veterans, who have no use for the account sign-up process anymore. The user can log into the site through the front page, by following a link to an interior page, or after the session has expired.

So there are many problems – namely, how to log into a site from many different places, with many different intentions. Each entry point can be solved in different ways. For the sake of consistency, using a pattern will work much better and make the product that much easier to learn. Let's make a pattern and apply it to this situation.

- **First**, *define the problem*, accounting for as many situations as possible. Defining the problem shouldn't take more than a few sentences.
- **Second**, *outline why that poses a problem* and list the situations where it commonly occurs. Start discussing potential solutions. This should be written as concisely as possible, and shouldn't be more than a page or two.
- **Third**, *propose an abstracted, reusable solution*, which shouldn't take more than a paragraph. It may be useful, in patterns concerning code or graphic design, to include sample graphics, wireframes, or pseudocode. But in most situations, you should have an essay that straddles the line between functional specification and mission statement. It says *here is how we will address this problem*, in any situation where it occurs.
- **Last**, *draw a diagram expressing the solution*. If it can't be expressed visually, it isn't a pattern.

Pseudocode is a rough, written description of how code should behave.

Returning to our example, here's how the pattern addressing the login problem would look when finished:

The user needs a way to authenticate from any location.

First-time users enter through the front page, and sign up for an account there. We don't need to account for the tiny percentage who enter through other pages, but veteran users who already have accounts need a way to easily log in from any page, including the front, and start working as fast as possible.

Login and account creation should be kept separate. Two separate groups of users access each section. Once a user has created an account, he shifts from the group needing to create an account into the group needing to authenticate using their new account.

Once logged in, users should be automatically directed to the original page they were trying to access. The login form should look identical on the front page and interior pages. Lastly, account creation should be kept slightly more prominent on the front page, because that's how new users will begin to interact with the site.

In this example, the bold statements describe the problem and solution, respectively.

I've kept the solution general. If you were writing this for yourself, you might want to be more specific, describing the specific layout of a login form, its cosmetics, and its behavior (i.e., whether caps lock is detected, whether the form automatically completes its fields, whether the login requires a second authentication step, whether there's a REMEMBER ME check box, whether account creation requires a confirmation email, whether a CAPTCHA is needed, etc). There's a lot to keep track of, with countless solutions for what looks on the surface like a simple feature. Write what best describes and solves *your* problem.

HOW TO USE PATTERNS.

Existing patterns are easy to find. Just searching online for the term "design patterns" gives you pattern libraries and books in many subject areas.

If you've already made your own patterns, or if you're consulting libraries of patterns that you find inspiring, you may ask yourself how they can be used when they amount to piecemeal, if detailed, requirements in a functional specification.

- **First**, *compile enough patterns* that they fully describe the product you're making. This sounds daunting, but the majority of the work is done for you by other libraries. Your problems probably aren't as unique as you think. Chances are that other people have experienced them, and written

---

This is how it's done in *A Pattern Language* as well.

A **CAPTCHA**, an acronym for "Completely Automated Public Turing test to tell Computers and Humans Apart," is a means of differentiating humans from robots when filling out forms to create accounts, leave comments on blogs, buy tickets, etc. Usually it involves solving a simple math problem, or typing a scrambled-up picture of words.

This section is heavily inspired by an essay by Ryan Singer, "An Introduction to Using Patterns in Web Design," Signal vs. Noise, http://37signals.com/papers/introtopatterns/ . For an application of this process to the creation of a building and a town, check out Christopher Alexander, *Notes on the Synthesis of Form* (Harvard University Press), where the idea of patterns is expanded on at great length.

and grouped patterns to solve them. These provide a great starting point that you can customize to your own situation.

Once you have your patterns together, you can use the rest of this process to design each step. Repeat it for other steps.

- **Second**, *list every element, needed actions of those elements, and the user's potential attitudes that exist at a given step.* In the case of the login pattern earlier, you could apply it to the front page or an interior page, which may require slightly different organization. *Label each element with a number.*
- **Third**, *group these numbers according to which elements affect each other directly.* For example, consider whether a login blank and a password blank would affect each other. One element may belong to many groups. *Label each grouping with a letter.*
- **Fourth**, *prioritize each group* based on its importance. You should have only three to five priority levels here - low, medium, and high will usually do.
- **Fifth**, *sketch mockups that correspond to each letter group*, in descending order of priority. Assume that these groups comprise separate interfaces. It's smart to work through this step on paper, so that you can erase and rewrite quickly.

  Most importantly, this step is where your pattern library comes in. If the library is well curated, then you should have answers for many common problems. Organizing your interface in this way frames it as a collection of patterns, because patterns are most applicable to common, sensible agglomerations of elements. Apply your patterns as they pertain to each group, and see how they affect your original concept of the layout and behavior.
- **Last**, *combine each sketch into a rough design.* Move the sketches around so they form a layout that makes logical and hierarchical sense.

Patterns move you from idea gathering to a promising wireframe that can be useful and beautiful once designed, coded, and polished. A less tangible benefit results as well: you can use patterns to defend your decisions in a more forceful and trusworthy way.

2.7. Employ natural mappings between controls and functions.

How is the relationship between elements and behavior and defined? Through a **mapping**, which connects a series of elements to each element's respective control. For instance, a light switch is mapped to a given light bulb. Easy enough, but how

The term "natural mapping" was coined by Don Norman in his seminal work *The Design of Everyday Things* (Doubleday Business). He devised the stove example.

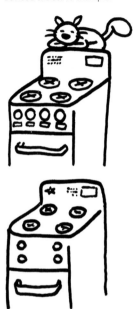

Sometimes the product is itself a platform, but most things you make are subservient to one.

does this scale? A row of light switches may turn on various lights, or groups of lights, in a large room. How do you know what switch affects what group?

Natural mappings are a subset of mappings where a set of functions is described by an identically organized set of controls. Natural mappings are a fundamental way to break down a cognitive barrier between the user and a product.

Consider a stove's burners and knobs. In the diagram at left, the burners don't naturally map to the stove: the burners are arranged in a 2 × 2 square, while the knobs are arranged in a 1 × 4 row. This layout is common to modern stoves.

The knobs can be reorganized without losing much surface area. In the below diagram, there's no ambiguity as to which knob controls which burner. One benefit of the new arrangement is we can remove the labels next to each knob, since the function of each knob is now self-evident. This would cost about the same to build as a poorly mapped stove, and it makes for a safer stove that wastes less natural gas, because people will make fewer errors.

Natural mappings can be used in more complex functionality than the on/off control of a stove. One instance is the columns of an audio mixing console. Each column of controls corresponds to a different input channel. If each column is labeled correctly, there's no ambiguity as to what treble knob changes what input. Scaling up to 32 or 64 channels (as with many professional mixers) is much less difficult when organized this way, and much easier to learn when the mapping is used universally across brands and types of mixers.

2.8. The context of your interface should prescribe its norms.

All objects have context. A product's context should dictate its appearance and behavior.

A **platform** is the operating system or device on which your product runs. A platform acts as the frame for your product. A game console is a platform; a controller or game is designed according to its constraints. A cell phone is a platform; headsets and applications are made for it. The personal computer is a platform; operating systems are written for it, which are themselves platforms; and programs are written for the platform of the operating system. A **system** is an interconnected set of platforms - operating system, input devices, central processor, screen, etc - that a user interacts with.

A product's context prescribes the way that it should work. An element's context prescribes the way that it should appear and behave. The subservience of a product to its platform and system is its **normative context**.

If the product is software written for a given operating system, for example, it should use conventions similar to other programs written for that operating system. It's likely that the operating system's developer has published a set of interface guidelines to aid you. If the product is a peripheral for a computer, it should connect to the computer with the appropriate protocol. If it's a website, many specifications exist to dictate good coding, usability, and accessibility practices, and you should develop with them in mind.

The World Wide Web Consortium (w3c) dictates most coding specifications on the web. For more information, check out http://w3.org.

People call products "Mac-like" or "Windows-like" depending on what how well they fit their parent operating system. Designers and users alike want the programs they use to look and behave like their respective systems, and they don't want to enter a separate, proprietary world with every new application that they open.

Human interface guidelines are published by hardware and software developers to dictate the norms of applications running on all common devices and operating systems. Search for the human interface guidelines for your specific operating system to read more.

How to design *like* your platform is impossible to define generally, because it differs from platform to platform. But as a platform gains traction among developers, and programs are lauded as examples of quality design, a body of knowledge and consensus emerges about how best to adapt to the ethos of your platform's stewards.

A recent example. Four months after programmers were allowed to develop third-party software for the iPhone, John Gruber wrote:

Figure out the absolute least you need to do to implement the idea, do just that, and then polish the hell out of the experience.

John Gruber, "iPhone-Likeness," Daring Fireball, http://daringfireball.net/2008/11/iphone_likeness .

He then set forth five principles that apply to "nearly every iPhone app designed by Apple, and … the ones [he likes] most from the App Store."

It's encouraging to see solid principles coming out of an entirely new interaction model in such a short period of time. It suggests that people will continue talking about future systems in this way.

Another example: in the beginning of the web, the HTML and CSS specifications were the subject of considerable debate. A decade or so later, people began using JavaScript frameworks to build application-like functionality. Further debates emerged.

In all parts of technology, new ways of doing things emerge, and then ways to do those things *well* emerge shortly after. The tools briefly precede the craft. Then new tools arrive. Given the recent pace of technological development, the whole process repeats so quickly that we don't have the chance to step back

Ishmael Reed, *Mumbo Jumbo* (Scribner), 218.

and notice it. Ishmael Reed concludes his novel *Mumbo Jumbo* with this: "Time is a pendulum. Not a river. More akin to what goes around comes around." Indeed.

EXAMPLES OF GOOD FIT IN CONTEXT.

Responding to normative context gives your product **good fit**, or the perception that it's a natural extension of the platform and system. Good fit responds naturally to common user behavior and affords a task as comfortably as possible. If a product has good fit, people will be happier to use it.

For example, new ergonomic keyboards tend to have good fit, while thick, boxy old keyboards have bad fit. One leads to repetitive stress injuries much faster than the other. Likewise, brick cell phones of the late eighties have substantially worse fit than current designs of cell phones, because of their size, weight, and feel.

One of the best descriptions of fit comes from Christopher Alexander. In *A Pattern Language*, he describes a pattern to build a seat that's attached to a wall:

Christopher Alexander, *A Pattern Language* (Oxford University Press), 925-6.

Before you build the seat, get hold of an old arm chair or a sofa, and put it into the position where you intend to build a seat. Move it until you really like it. Leave it there for a few days. See if you enjoy sitting in it. Move it if you don't. When you have got it into a position which you like, and where you often find yourself sitting, you know it is a good position. Now build a seat that is just as wide, and just as well padded – and your built-in seat will work.

Common sense, but rarely applied; we tend to put these sorts of decisions in the hands of those who may not fully understand what we need.

WHAT TO DO ABOUT IT.

Because one's operating system prescribes the norms of its applications, it's easy for users to determine whether a program looks and behaves like others. Furthermore, familiarity correlates with trustworthiness. No matter how well the program is designed, if people think that it doesn't fit with the operating system, then they'll conclude that the program is *poorly* designed.

Don't try to squeeze something into an operating system where it doesn't belong. Instead, change the product so that it fits better. Hardware *and* software should be integrated in design and function.

Software can have extremely poor fit in certain contexts. For example, cross-platform programming languages promise easy and cheap deployability at the cost of incoherent aesthetics, bloated code, and degraded performance. Countless products have been developed with elements and behavior that belong to no system, with characterless graphics and – almost by definition – unacceptably long response times.

Cross-platform technology fails because no context *can* prescribe its norms, since it refuses to adapt to its contexts. It tries to please everybody, and in doing so pleases nobody. Exceptions to this rule occur only by accident.

Very few users regularly encounter platforms with small market share anymore: everyone uses one of a handful of systems for web browsing, operating systems, computer hardware, and mobile phones. As a result, increasingly many developers shun cross-platform technology, instead developing products for only a couple of the most popular platforms.

While I'm not fond of monopolies, and while it can be argued that imposing the norms of an operating system is isolationist and stifling of the designer's means of expression, maybe this sort of consensus is what's needed for the most reliable experiences, lessening the risk of a breakdown between developer and user. Norms affect one's experience with an entire platform, and in doing so, they honor the intent of the platform's creators.

2.8.1. *Use traditional elements instead of custom ones.*

Users appreciate the familiar in their interfaces. When they know where something is and what it does, it's easier for them to complete tasks with it. Conversely, every time a non-traditional element appears, they have to expend mental effort to understand its purpose and function.

The context of your product should determine its aesthetics. If an operating system provides pre-made buttons to drop into your application, then creating a different kind of button will confuse the user. Always use the system-provided button. When developing a website, use actual HTML for text, instead of text saved as an image.

Never create an element that has already been created for you by the platform's creators. Standard elements are the building blocks of your product's visual and behavioral language.

2.8.2. Replace traditional elements only if there is a functional purpose for doing so.

Often, you'll find that your platform and system don't have the ability to sufficiently describe your product's desired features. In this case, it's reasonable to replace traditional elements with ones that you've created.

Appearance is not the same as function. Don't replace traditional elements to fit a graphic design or branding campaign; only do so if you need to create new utility that the system can't sufficiently provide on its own.

2.8.3. Information is molded by where it is displayed.

The portions of *Cadence & Slang* about information display owe an enormous debt to the work of Edward Tufte. His four books, *The Visual Display of Quantitative Information*, *Envisioning Information*, *Visual Explanations*, and *Beautiful Evidence* (Graphics Press) have redefined common perceptions of data display.

Context determines the way that your product displays qualitative information (anecdotal evidence, words, ideas) and quantitative information (numbers, data). In each case, your platform may imply an optimal scale, layout, behavior, typography, or data-ink ratio. Following these guides makes data more readable and honest.

That said, the normative context of information is sometimes the product itself, not the product's platform or system. Ignoring the product affects information's scale and meaning. Good interaction design involves understanding how and where to mold information to fit its layout - and which context it's appropriate to mold it to.

In the case of data plots, there's considerable research favoring certain design standards to make information more readable and honest:

- The cause should be on the x-axis, and the effect should be on the y-axis.
- If you're working with Latin text, labels should read from left to right, like normal text in a book - not vertically or upside-down.
- The width-to-height ratio should lie between the golden ratio (approximately 1.414 : 1) and the golden section (φ : 1, or approximately 1.618 : 1).
- Most quantitative plots should be wider than they are tall, and they shouldn't be excessively short on one side so it's easier to read the other's axis.

If your data won't fit elegantly, it's better to rework the design to fit the data. Don't carelessly put the data somewhere that it doesn't belong.

The interactive data displays on journalism sites are great examples of designing to fit data well. Hovering over areas of maps pops up information about given locations. Hovering and clicking graphs explains the details of a narrative. Almost all of these displays lie separate from any sort of *text*-based story. Many are posted as their own features.

Or consider stock quotes on financial trackers. In most cases, financial data display is the entire product; no frame is necessary for the data, because *the entire page* qualifies as quantitative information, organized and displayed to imply a narrative. Sliders exist to alter scale; contextual flags explain sudden changes in value. As a user hovers over parts of the graph, market capitalization, closing price, and share volume dance in a sidebar.

On the opposite end are **sparklines**: intricate, word-sized graphics that can fit into a paragraph of text to describe appropriate short-term time narratives.

For more on sparklines, see 6.4.1.

Displayed in the right way, data is capable of telling these dense and complex narratives, and it deserves the same attention as any other part of your product.

2.9. Input devices should fit the function and the person equally.

I can't run the 100-meter dash as quickly as an Olympic sprinter can, but I can probably hold things with a stronger grip than my 88-year-old grandmother. My vision is about 20/30, which is worse than my sister but better than my father.

Human factors is the science of discovering the variance of human capability and applying it to the things that we use. The human factors of your platform's hardware should fit well with your users and the tasks that they're trying to perform.

Touch screens are less appropriate for precise drawing than stylus tablets, especially for the fat-fingered. Qwerty layouts are more appropriate than Dvorak for the vast majority of computer users who haven't bothered to learn Dvorak. Voice recognition doesn't work for issuing all but the simplest commands in the quietest environments, and therefore it's hardly appropriate for cities, though its capabilities may improve in the future.

Affordances.

James J. Gibson, *The Ecological Approach to Visual Perception* (Psychology Press).

For more on affordances, especially as they pertain to software, see 6.1.1.

Psychologist James J. Gibson defined an **affordance** as "an action possibility inherent to a given environment or object;" or what something allows you to do (or not do) with it.

We go through our whole lives taking advantage of various affordances without consciously realizing it. Think of the cantilevered handle on a tea kettle that automatically opens the spout when you pick it up. Or the transit card with a notch in the corner and a hole in the bottom that imply the correct way to insert it into the turnstile. Or shovels with long handles that give us more leverage to move heavy loads of snow. Or custom-molded grips for potato peelers. Or a corkscrew, redesigned so it grips the bottle and pierces the cork with almost no mechanical effort.

Affordances allow us to work with the world more easily. They adapt objects to us. But affordances that work for some people may not work for others: if you design a steep staircase, for example, an adult can climb it more quickly, but a small child cannot.

Make sure that your product affords the right things for the right people. If you're designing hardware, ask yourself if the buttons are easy to press, if the device is easy to grip, if things are laid out and formed in a way that ergonomically and naturally fits our capability. If you're designing software, ask yourself if buttons are easy to find and click, if it's possible to run through forms quickly, if their layouts imply functional clarity.

2.10. *Provide for disabled users.*

Don't alienate people because their needs are incompatible with your priorities. Using a full-page Flash application for your website excludes the blind, who rely on screen readers. Using 8-pixel-tall text with no obvious way to change its size doesn't account for users with vision impairment. These are only two of the many ways that the world can further marginalize those with disabilities.

Section 508's official site is http://www.section508.gov.

For more on international accessibility guidelines on the web , a list exists courtesy of the W3C at http://www. w3.org/WAI/Policy/ .

Countless agencies try to make technology more accessible. In the United States, the Americans with Disabilities Act (ADA) provides legal incentive to create accessible products. Section 508 pertains to both software and hardware, with guidelines that are applicable to anything you create. Other countries have adopted similar measures.

We owe it to ourselves and our society to develop and support accessible interfaces. Simplicity and clarity get us close, but they're no substitute for a continued, conscious effort.

3.1. Find the simplest complete solution.

Products should be simple. Simple products are easier for developers to maintain, and easier and more fun for people to use. By reducing the number of required steps in a task, incrementally disclosing information, eliminating redundant content, and hiding complexity where it's impossible to eliminate it entirely, we move closer to the ideal of instinctual usability.

There is an essential tension between **simplicity**, which is the thoughtful reduction of unnecessary elements; and **completeness**, which is to have enough function to be useful. Products must remain functionally complete to their fundamental tasks. The product must do precisely enough, and its creators must know where and when to stop.

You can't easily make a complex product into a simple one, but you can try to convey the feeling that it is. The impression of simplicity is powerful on its own, and functions well as a compromise.

It's also possible to oversimplify, so that products lack usefulness. Removing *essential* features will force users into unexpected situations, leaving them unable to understand how to operate the product. Removing *inessential* features illuminates and strengthens paths.

3.2. Be clean.

Here, something is **clean** when the ratio of ink or pixels dedicated to *function* is maximized relative to that dedicated to *form*. But since this can be qualitative, it's hard to formulate a process to enforce it in interfaces. The well-trained interaction designer knows it when he sees it.

In the world of information display, Edward Tufte coined the terms *data-ink* and *chartjunk,* advocating to maximize the data-ink ratio by erasing and lightening axes, eliminating (or lightening) trend lines and grids, and removing anything inessential to perceiving the information. Technology would benefit from adopting the same sentiment.

We can go further, though. It's useful to differentiate between true cleanliness and perceptual cleanliness. In real life, we assume a room is clean when it promotes the appearance of well-scrubbed counter tops, vacuumed carpets, inoffensive odor, and lack of clutter. But if you hide a bunch of crap underneath the flap of your sofa, your room only *looks* clean.

Cleanliness should pervade your product, front to back. The code *and* the appearance should be clean. If code is reused, take

3:

Simplicity & Clarity

The simplest complete solution is first referenced in Alan Cooper, *About Face* (Wiley).

3.7 expands further on this idea.

advantage of object-oriented programming to repurpose it. If code can be made more readable and elegant without negatively affecting the product's performance, clean it up.

Elements should be unambiguously placed. The layout shouldn't be crowded, or have too much white space. Using traditional elements gives the user the perception of cleanliness by virtue of familiarity. Clean products have instantaneously recognizable function.

JUSTIFYING THE EXISTENCE OF ELEMENTS.

All elements should have **roles** associated with them: in other words, they should have some functional purpose within the product. Everything that you add to a product should be justified in terms of its appearance, location, and behavior. Periodically audit every detail of the layout for its purpose:

- *"This vertical divider is here to separate the search form from the login form."*
- *"This button is here because the user needs a mechanism to reset their custom page settings."*
- *"This text area is here, in this size, to encourage feedback."*

If you can't justify an element's existence, remove it.

TRADITIONAL ELEMENTS.

For more about traditional elements, see 2.8.1 and 2.8.2.

Using the elements that your normative context prescribes helps to ensure the feeling of cleanliness because the creators of your platform - be they the programmers of your operating system or the designers of your hardware - usually put considerable thought into creating basic elements that get out of your way as much as possible.

NEGATIVE SPACE.

For more on negative space, see 2.2. For more on arranging elements consistently and simply, see 6.3.3.

Negative space should be consistent and generous. Let the elements on your canvas breathe, so that they can differentiate themselves from each other as much as possible, allowing for no ambiguity and more clarity.

MEANINGFUL HIERARCHY.

One of the best ways to discover the hierarchy of elements is through applying a pattern language. For more on pattern languages, check out section 2.6.

The meaning of your interface is implied by the arrangement of its elements. Establishing a hierarchy of what's important on a page indicates what features matter the most. It also defines elements better, conveying the product's broader theme.

On websites, hierarchy can be established on a global level with site maps, and on a per-page level with layout tweaks that follow users' reading patterns.

In any product, hierarchy can be established by emphasizing (or de-emphasizing) specific elements. This leads the user's eye in a more focused way than with a layout where all the type is the same size, face, and weight.

Hierarchy can also be established by grouping elements, and emphasizing (or de-emphasizing) the groups.

FEATURE CREEP.

Feature creep is what happens when unnecessary features are added to a product before it ships. Sometimes marketing or sales departments want to boost a product's specifications. Many stakeholders may try to push through various concepts for an otherwise simple product, and they compromise by implementing all of them.

Simple products are easier to learn, and cluttering them is difficult to undo once any new features have gained traction. Simple products have to resist feature creep in any form, and you have to be firm in saying no to any suggestions that may not satisfy the majority of your audience.

3.3. *Eliminate excess graphics.*

Graphics are tremendously useful for establishing and reinforcing branding, offering a consistent experience, and promoting a fit and finish in the final product. But graphics shouldn't replace traditional elements unless there's a functional reason for it; and graphics shouldn't overwhelm the product, because that risks distracting the user.

Interactions should be kept separate from graphic design. Only use graphics if they fulfill a functional purpose, contributing to the product's interactive character. Any graphics used for their own sake should be removed.

Disputes should favor the conventional and familiar, the tried and tested. In a world where everyone is trying to shout loudly, simplicity and elegance speak forcefully.

Scattered and grouped elements.

Sections 1.7 through 1.9 discuss feature sets, and developing for intermediate users, in greater detail.

1.15 discusses why resisting complexity is important as your organization scales.

Paul Rand, *A Designer's Art* (Yale University Press), 213:

In the frantic hope of "standing out," he tries to outshout, outcolor, and outglitter his competitor. He approves gaudy color schemes, oversized or misshapen lettering embellished with outlines, double or triple shadows, pseudo-Victorian decorations, and other exhibitionistic devices.

Thinner and lighter lines.

Frequently, borders, grids, and graphs are too thick or too dark. Lightening and thinning these directs users' attention to the content, which then encourages them to understand and interact with it.

Background and foreground.

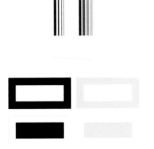

Calming the background of any interface helps draw attention to the elements that you want people to see. The background connects with all elements at once, which drastically affects users' impressions.

Custom buttons.

Buttons are one of the most common controls. You should follow the context of your platform or system when creating them. The shape and size of buttons should be determined by context first, and their relative importance second.

Be sensitive to using iconography on buttons. Icons should universally imply the right function. For example, using an icon of a floppy disk to describe a save command no longer makes any sense: nobody uses floppy disks anymore, and many people have *never* used them. There are many potential alternatives, including a text label.

Combining text and icon in one button is a good way to train the user in the meaning of the icon, while providing a larger target for the user to trigger. It may be useful to provide the option to view just text or just icon in a product's preferences.

Legal copy.

Keep legal copy out of the way whenever possible. Move it into a separate page, away from the interaction. Word it in plain, simple, unambiguous language whenever you can.

If your product requires authorization of a contract at setup, don't force the user to scroll to the bottom, or require a minimum time limit before the OK button becomes pliant.

Advertising.

If it exists in your product, advertising is necessarily part of the user's interaction. If you alter a product with any advertising, you are making design decisions. Advertising should be trustworthy, pertinent, not subversive, and out of the way of the interaction.

Advertising is sensitive ground; users hate being marketed to, especially if it gets in the way of their task. It's vitally important to maintain the trust of your users when advertising to them – and especially when advertising products outside your control. Users know when they're being marketed to rather than being given actual content. Poorly executed advertising builds frustration and distrust as it wastes the user's time – and one day, the negative impressions will build up enough that people will stop using your product.

LOGOS AND BRANDING.

Branding should imply the meaning of your product. Keep it as simple as possible; the best logos are intensely expressive with only a few elements, and can survive harsh printing conditions and poor screen resolutions. Many successful brands don't even directly discuss the product itself.

For more on logo design, take a look at Per Mollerup, *Marks of Excellence* (Phaidon).

3.4. Employ a neutral and balanced color palette.

Color should be deployed with the same care as any other aspects of the product. Just as you shouldn't use ten shades of the same color when only three shades would do, the colors you *do* choose to use should be neutral and harmonious with each other. Bold colors and stark contrasts should be used sparingly. Eliminate any colors that clash, that perturb the eye in ways unrelated to the product's function.

Consider the ways that color can vary:

MANY COLORS.

BRIGHT COLORS.

DISSONANT COLORS.

CONSONANT COLORS.

MUTED COLORS.

FEW COLORS; FEW HUES.

Which of these palettes is easier on the eyes? Which is harder? What do these colors say when in context with one another? Or, for example:

versus

These contain the same four colors in different proportions. The narrower orange bar implies that it's more of an accent color. This mutes the color palette, with more sparing saturation. The amount that each color is used in practice matters as much as its value.

3.5. Omit needless words.

Words should only exist if they fit the product's purpose. Long, opaque words should be replaced with short, simple ones. Excess words should be cut out entirely. And all supplementary documentation should lie outside where the user works.

One way to omit needless words is to speak as much of the interface out loud as possible. If any sentences or fragments sound clunky or awkward, the user will think so too. Another way is to surround any problematic fragments in brackets. Then, go back through the product and find ways to replace those areas with shorter substitutes, or eliminate them entirely.

At first, it's likely that you'll frequently call out text, in longer chunks. But as you practice this skill, you'll find yourself writing more concisely and clearly - and striking out less.

Let's return to some of the error messages that I cited in 2.3.6, and rewrite them to be as concise as possible.

The application [application name] quit unexpectedly. [The operating system] and other applications are not affected. Click Relaunch to launch the application again. Click Report to see more details or send a report to [the developer].

Sorry, [application name] crashed unexpectedly. If you were not doing anything confidential (entering passwords or other private information), you can help to improve the application by reporting the problem.

Both of these could be reworded as "[application name] quit unexpectedly. An anonymous error report has been sent."

Beta-only warning message - not to be localized: UMESSAGE *buffer full! Should never happen. Generate fewer messages.*

"Sorry, but the message buffer is full."

An unhandled error occurred in the GUI, *further errors may be reported. -6*

Rewording this to "Graphical error" or "Rendering error" is descriptive, accurate, and doesn't cause more worries.

Alan Cooper, *About Face* (Wiley), 162:

> A program may be bold or timid, colorful or drab, but it should be so for a specific, goal-directed reason.

This is also a pretty good thing to do when writing a book.

This technique is indebted to William Zinsser, *On Writing Well* (Collins).

If you ever took a writing class, you will probably recognize this rule. This comes verbatim from William Strunk and E.B. White, *The Elements of Style* (Longman); in many ways, "omit needless words" is a distillation of that entire book.

Strunk says writing should have no needless words or sentences "for the same reason that a drawing should have no unnecessary lines and a machine no unnecessary parts," which is so pertinent to this book that it's almost clairvoyant. Strunk also advocates the active voice over the passive one, and positive writing over negative - true when writing for any products.

See also 2.3 for why a positive tone is essential in writing for technology.

*[application name] did not shutdown tidily. Check /home/user/.
appname/logs/save for diagnostic log files and consider reporting
them to the [application name] team if this is the result of an
application error. Also check the Wiki (see the Help menu) for
"[application name] Disappears"*

This doesn't help the user, and should be eliminated entirely.

3.6. Keep transitions short.

Animations keep the interaction fluid from step to step, teach-
ing the user what to expect as they proceed. Executed well, animations can be useful and expressive, but there are many ways
to put animation in the way. Keeping them short - under 100
milliseconds, and at a high frame rate - helps ensure that they
won't get in the way. They should change from the first state to
the second without irrelevant content in between.

It's telling that some of the best interaction design and user
experience companies - Apple most famous among them - have
begun hiring designers with animation or motion video experience. Operating systems now use animations to minimize
and close windows, scroll through menus, and track progress.
Smartphones have employed animations to open applications,
delete items in a list, and email photos. And while animations
aren't essential, they provide utility and beauty.

3.7. Eliminate chartjunk.

As implied in 3.3 and 3.5, the rule "omit needless words" applies
equally to graphics. So it is with data, too.

Presented with clarity, data is a narrative. It tells stories, and
sometimes the stories are just as riveting as those set to prose.
Data is often considered boring, but it's only boring if you have
a boring story to tell - or if you tell it boringly.

Edward Tufte coined the term **chartjunk** in *The Visual Display
of Quantitative Information* (Graphics Press) as any elements that
don't aid in the comprehension of data. So eliminating chartjunk leaves the designer with the essence of data, called **data-
ink:** a scale, points, and some implied relationship. It mutes
color; it erases liberally.

Eliminating chartjunk to highlight data-ink provides many
benefits. It's faster to display, easier on the eyes, and more un-
derstandable by the user. It casts data display in the same context as the rest of the interface: a spare layout forms the frame
that dictates the context of its data within.

Tackling chartjunk in practice. Here are some example graphs, pulled from Brian Venn, "Render dynamic graphs in SVG," IBM developerWorks, http://www.ibm.com/developerworks/xml/library/x-svggrph/, with my redesigns:

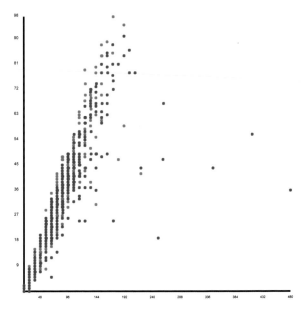

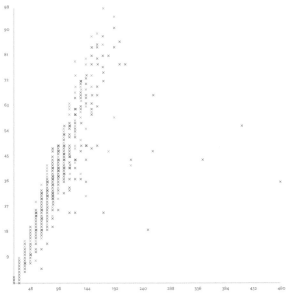

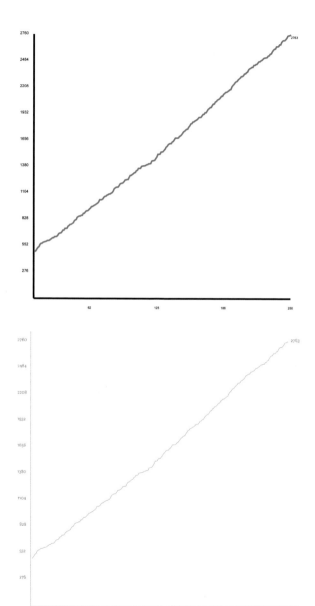

3.8. *Replace metaphors with abstractions.*

Technology is reductive. It simplifies the real and the tangible into something that is both machine- and human-readable. This process is called **abstraction**. It begins with something real, something that's *only* human-readable: handwriting, typing on a calculator, placing a phone call, or turning on a TV, for example. Then you remove elements from it, moving towards the essence of the original idea, towards simplicity. It stops somewhere in between, where the original concept fits the machine's context in a way that remains recognizable to us.

Consider the essential functions of a given device. For example, what does a TV remote *need* to do? Turn the TV on and off, certainly. Change channel and volume. Beyond these essential functions, anything else can be argued as excess, including more complicated ways to accomplish these tasks.

Metaphors are anathema to this process. Using a picture of a desk to represent a desktop, a three-dimensional rendering of an office for an office application, a dog or snooty butler that fetches search results, or an anthropomorphic paperclip that yells at you every time you create a new document, does not make a task simple. They all distract the user, who thinks: "What on earth is a butler going to do to help me search?"

It's tempting to think that literal metaphors make a product more familiar and inviting. But there are many other ways to make interfaces inviting, and many familiar tropes of GUI design – how to use a mouse, or where menu panes are located – have already been taken as axioms. Worse yet, real-world metaphors could be interpreted as condescension by any intermediate or expert users – and those are usually the first people who buy your product.

For more on context, see 2.8. Making an interface graphically and functionally simple, with basic tasks abstracted in ways that are familiar to your product's context, should remove the need for any metaphors.

3.9. *Eliminate title popups and splash screens.*

Splash screens waste users' time and get in the way of their tasks. Nobody wants to see a prompt that introduces something that they know they've already opened. Additionally, many platforms and systems have built-in ways to show that your program or website is loading, which removes the need for you to implement that yourself.

Some platforms require that your product have a startup screen. If so, you should display the product's blank slate.

3.10. *Only require account creation when it provides a clear benefit to the user.*

Sometimes products will ask you to register them at the first launch. Others will have you create an account on the company's website to get access to updates and news.

Accounts' benefits should connect with how the product works. For example, if you're releasing a GPS tool that tracks users' whereabouts, it makes sense to require an account to tie their identity to their progress. Or if making a web-based task manager, then accounts are the best way to access data.

If mandatory account creation only benefits you, for marketing or research purposes, then it's just as useless as the splash screen. If you're using accounts to mine demographic data, there are much better ways to accomplish that: for example, surveying some users every year will give you broad ideas about who is using your product in the long term. And if you require account creation because that data will earn money, then you should question whether the need to make money outweighs the frustration that you will give users by requiring something that they perceive as needless and intrusive.

3.11. *Create real interfaces.*

Simplicity applies to your design process. Creating real interfaces as quickly as possible reduces the number of steps in your work, and it builds consensus more quickly. A working prototype is the most useful kind of functional specification, and it should be sought out.

Functional specifications and wireframes don't accurately reflect the final product. They're often discarded early in the process, and at worst they're continually fought over.

Sketches are great precursors to real world design, because they address layout and hierarchy concerns very quickly. But a sketch doesn't describe any behavior. This can be solved through storyboarding many sketches, but that rarely scales to larger products with many steps. It makes more sense to build something workable; then behavior can be determined.

Finally, design should pervade every single stage of the development process. Design can take an early role through sketching and brainstorming. Then, building something real gives more form to your ideas: something with accurate shape and fit, to solve future problems.

4.1. Understand the user's expectations.

Harvard Business School professor Theodore Levitt:

People don't want a quarter-inch drill, they want a quarter-inch hole.

4.1.1. Users view interfaces in terms of what they need to accomplish.

For a long time, the practice of making products easier to use was called **user-oriented design**. This pays attention to who users are – augmented with demographic research, contextual inquiry, and stakeholder interviews. People believed it important to understand potential users before we could understand what products to make.

Which it is, of course. But the starting point has changed. Many designers are now considering something called **goal-oriented design**. Through this, designs are framed in terms of the user's goals. We dictate the steps that users should go through to complete a task, and design from there.

A major premise behind goal-oriented design is that *users don't care about what makes technology work*. When users sit down with a computer, for example, they think "I need to send an email," not "I need to click these buttons in order to send an email." And when users see your product, they should say "it helps me deal with this problem I have."

They don't know what goes into making a computer or a cell phone. And they're right to do so: ultimately, it doesn't matter. The computer or the cell phone is a tool – and as computers become more prevalent, the focus has shifted towards fitting them into people's lives.

Many expert users believe that technology should be an end in itself – and experts tend to be the ones to develop new things. But this thinking corrupts the intent of products. We use technology to make life easier, but it adds complexity to our tasks. Why *would* people think about how a CPU is made? Why would *anyone*? What does it matter to our neighbors, to our families?

4.1.2. Know your audience.

Even though goals matter the most, you still can't make relevant products if you don't know your users and their desires. We create things based on what we know. And often, products are created when we have too little experience to understand users' needs.

4:

Managing expectations

The above quotation is from Clayton M. Christensen, Scott Cook, and Taddy Hall, "What Customers Want from Your Products," Harvard Business School Working Knowledge, http://hbswk. hbs.edu/item/5170.html .

This has also been referred to as *task-* or *action-oriented design*.

Consider the dot-com boom and bust from 1998 to 2001. It centered around San Francisco, a denser-than-par urban area with a rigorous street grid. Many of the resulting products focused on home delivery or e-commerce. The party line – you can get *anything you want* online! – was marketed to the entire country, even though most cities were not as dense or walkable, or with a street grid as likely to support such a large delivery infrastructure, as San Francisco. Many services in the first iteration of the web were incompatible with the way that most of America worked.

Many design problems, like this one, can be solved through **ethnographic research**, an academic technique of determining the cultural, aesthetic, and social values of a demographic by observing and interviewing them. When this is done right, you'll quickly discard bad ideas and focus on the good ones. Then you can refine those good ideas into an internally consistent mission. Combined with user testing, this forms the beginning of more ambitious designs.

4.1.3. *Know your technological context.*

What people use today will be obsolete tomorrow. Figure out what exists right now, what people like right now, and what people consider outdated.

4.1.4. *Know your expectational context.*

Users' beliefs are the sum of their past experiences. When someone works with a great interface, they consider future experiences in the context of that interface. And when they have bad experiences, future impressions of similar products are colored by that negative moment.

As our devices' capabilities improve, our expectations also change about what they can provide. Once people have worked with a better product than one they're used to, going back to the original product tends to make them more frustrated than had they stuck with the original product.

Finally, young users tend to figure out new interfaces faster than old users because they have fewer preconceptions about how that interface should work.

All of these factors need to be accounted for so we can make products that are as grounded as possible.

4.1.5. *Review current research.*

Understanding the pertinent research to your interface provides a tremendous amount of inspiration. Both in and out of academia, new ideas arise all the time. Related topics in cognitive psychology and social anthropology will help as well. Seek out the biggest library in your metro area. Spend a few weeks there; bury yourself in books.

Many private-sector companies, such as Xerox, Procter & Gamble, and Microsoft, have in-house research departments that publish their new findings to the design community at large.

4.1.6. *Avoid theoretical research.*

A lot of research disconnects designers from users, talking about notional future desires, and notional interfaces that could fit those desires. This is a great way to generate new ideas about interactions, it's inspiring for future design methods, and it's helpful to frame complex problems, but it's not so good for writing products that you want to ship today.

If you take advantage of theoretical research about concepts that are only tenable a few years from now, make sure you treat it with skepticism, understand all of its attendant limitations, and test rigorously.

4.1.7. *Avoid group research.*

Focus groups frequently suppress the will of the minority or the timid in favor of those who talked first, or are most gregarious. Sometimes they quash edge cases. Sometimes they push edge cases as if they were common. Regardless, they acknowledge group needs while downplaying individual beliefs.

4.1.8. Interview stakeholders.

Stakeholders are the people who design, develop, and market the product. If you work as an in-house designer, your stakeholders are any coworkers affiliated directly with what you're designing. If you're a consultant or freelancer, your stakeholders are the employees of your client.

Stakeholders have strong opinions on the project's financial, programmatic, and logistic constraints, and they can assess whether your ideas gel with the company's mission. Taken in sum, their opinions represent the company's goals and conditions, and the relationships between the two.

It takes practice and fine-tuned diplomacy to negotiate with stakeholders. Organizations are often thorny, complicated, full of power struggles. The people you work with could be several levels of management away from those who give final approval. Or the decision makers could be close by, but stay silent until after the work has been done.

Regardless, you need to understand the business that you work with. Interview as many people as it takes to gather a complete portrait of the way that the organization works.

Some stakeholder roles.

- *Executives* run the company. They're the best to talk to about the company's intangible aspects, the large-scale vision that inspires employees and gives them the drive to work well. They're also good to consult about the structure of the company, as well as its competitors.
- *Product managers*, who keep design and engineering on track, act as **subject matter experts**. Their input can inform much of the product's functionality. Subject matter experts are

well-versed in not only your product, but the context that surrounds it: the industry, its competitors.
- *Engineers* write and test the product's code.
- *Designers* determine how the front end will look. They'll be able to talk about the history of the brand, and what cosmetic decisions they'd like to make.
- *Quality assurance* (QA) tests the code that engineers write – and, in organizations that prioritize design, they also test your recommended interactions.
- *Marketers* brand the product. They'll also know a lot about the state of the product's brand identity.
- *Salespeople* pitch the product to customers. They'll know what goes into purchasing decisions, why people support the product, and why they may gravitate towards competitors.
- *Technical support* follows up with customers after the product is purchased.

Each of these roles provides you with a unique set of challenges, but all of them require compassionate and even-handed responses to oft-contentious views. In the end, the best thing that you can have on your side is practice.

Conducting the interview.

It helps to conduct stakeholder interviews with two people: one to lead the interview, and one to record the stakeholder's responses. Ask stakeholders what their role is, who the product is intended for, what constraints they're operating in, what they want to do for the project, and what the product should accomplish.

Many of the answers to these questions may be different from what you expect. Moreover, everyone has opinions about design, even if they aren't trained in the subject. Find ways to account for these in your own decisions.

Specific questions vary from role to role:

- When interviewing executives, ask about the timeline, as well as what trade-offs they're willing to make if the timeline can't be hit perfectly.
- When interviewing product managers, ask what the product's most common demographic is, what differences exist between user roles, and the product's desired features.
- When interviewing engineers, ask what technological decisions have been made, what the product's underlying archi-

tecture is (if one already exists), and how the current product works in basic terms (if it exists).

- When interviewing quality assurance, ask how they work with engineers to find and fix bugs, and how they'll conduct testing on this particular product.
- When interviewing marketers, ask who they believe the company's users are, and how that will change; how the product fits into the company's strategy; what the product's brand identity or style guide looks like; and who the company's biggest competitors are.
- When interviewing salespeople, ask who they're going to pitch the product to, what differentiates your product over a competitor's, how sales are lost, and what potential customers ask about most frequently.
- When interviewing technical support, ask what the most frequent problems have been in similar products (if any), if they have any ideas for fixing those problems, and how they plan to triage future cases for this product – whether their process is set to change.

4.1.9. *Interview users.*

With stakeholder interviews, you gather a portrait of the company making the product. With user interviews, you understand what people want to do with the product, and how it should function. Not all stakeholders are users, of course, and good designers know how to fit the square peg of user needs into the round hole of a company's interests and abilities.

Unless you're developing a product of considerable size, you don't need to conduct more than a half-dozen user interviews. While this is probably far fewer in number than your stakeholder interviews, they're just as important. You're there to create a product that fills their needs. They're the final arbiters, the ones who tell you whether you did your job well.

The balance between user and stakeholder interviews is discussed in 4.1.10.

Recruitment.

Recruitment can be daunting. First, you have to determine the criteria by which users can be recruited; then you have to make sure you find the right people to fit those criteria, which can be very exacting and particular; then you have to make them show up in person, which presents logistic challenges. For this reason, many firms outsource recruitment to third parties.

User interviews shouldn't last more than an hour – and if you're recruiting from the general public, you should probably offer some sort of honorarium to compensate for their time.

Conducting the interview.

Focus on understanding what tasks the user wants to complete. You'll ask what they do most frequently with the product, and what tasks are the most important. How do these tasks affect other people? Very few tasks are conducted in a vacuum.

If you're redesigning an existing product, ask about their current setup and figure out its benefits and shortcomings.

User interviews are opportunities to vent. Be patient and listen to what they have to say about the product's drawbacks.

When it comes to asking questions, our first impulse is to project our opinions. We want to agree with the user; we want to clarify their points. But this colors people's views, and it doesn't allow us to understand what they have to say. We have to suppress this and encourage people to provide their own thoughts. Questions should be open-ended, asking the user what they are trying to do, why they feel the way they do, and what they think they have to do to accomplish something.

We wouldn't have an interview in the first place if we knew what our users wanted. Interview people as if they're the teachers and we're the students. Towards that end, it's extremely important to be non-judgmental and humble. If they use our products in unexpected ways, we should be sympathetic to that and encourage them to expand on their own needs.

Questions should be deliberately naïve, asking about the greater context of the user's profession. That way, you don't make any assumptions about terms or processes that you may not know. We should ask for more detail when the user describes anything that we don't fully understand. It's always better to ask for clarification than to assume you can fill gaps in later. But you should mention that you plan to ask naïve questions up-front, especially with stakeholders. Otherwise, your interviewee may assume that you're clueless and inexperienced.

Finally, questions shouldn't ask the user for specific solutions. Finding the right answer is *your* job.

4.1.10. Judge stakeholder and user opinions equally.

If there's a conflict between what stakeholders want and what users want, then you should consider compromises that fill the desires of each equally, as if each group is represented by

Kim Goodwin says that this "is the product designer's equivalent of asking a patient where it hurts." Stakeholder and user interviews are discussed in much greater detail in chapters 5 through 8 of Goodwin's reference tome *Designing for the Digital Age* (Wiley).

You should only interview stakeholders as users if they're the only users.

a separate person, and you're trying to make both as happy as possible.

4.1.11. *Test your product at every stage of completion.*

Testing is the best way to ensure that your product works right. No amount of research can substitute for well-done testing. Because you can test products at any level of functionality or fidelity, it should start as soon as a prototype is put together.

Formal testing takes considerable money, effort, and time to conduct. In most cases, it takes so long that it diverts your focus away from making a great product. Hiring a full usability team, recruiting subjects from the general public, and buying fancy eye-tracking equipment are luxuries afforded by only the largest companies – and only if they really want to do usability testing, or if they have enough time to do it well. We're usually too busy for that – but the alternative, commonly referred to as **discount usability testing** or *guerilla usability,* offers little in compromise and considerable benefit in agility.

One of the fiercest advocates for unorthodox, economical testing methods is Jakob Nielsen. In the mid-nineties, he coined the terms *discount usability* and *guerilla HCI.* He was the first to run usability tests on sketched prototypes to isolate major problems as early as possible. He ventured these ideas twenty years ago, and they were poorly received at first.

Jakob Nielsen, "Discount Usability: 20 Years," Alertbox, http://www.useit.com/alertbox/discount-usability.html .

But fortunately, since then, discount testing has become respected in many organizations. It's affordable; it can be conducted faster; it offers immediate, actionable advice.

Only a tiny handful of interaction designers ever conduct professional usability testing. They might do it once in graduate school, and then dismiss it as a fluke of infinite resources, unbound by the constraints of time or budget.

But you can't forgo testing entirely. Done economically, testing becomes a feasible challenge, not a pipe dream.

USABILITY TESTING ON A BUDGET.

When most people refer to **usability testing,** they're talking about giving recruited users a series of tasks to accomplish on a product or prototype at any stage of completion, timing their responses, gauging their reaction, and asking them to explain their impressions.

For example, if you're making an email client, you may tell the user to check, compose, and send an email. If you're writing

Note that this is different from user interviews, which should take place *before* prototyping. But the principles that apply to interviews – not asking suggestive questions and listening carefully – still apply.

a scheduling application, you may want the user to create some events and check for time conflicts.

Usability tests time the user or count a task's steps to prove the effects of design decisions quantitatively. If the time (or number of steps) decreases to complete a task, we say that the product's usability has increased by that much. It's also useful to gauge a product's usability by the number of errors a user commits: the fewer, the more usable.

Usability tests need a way to ensure consistency between test subjects, and a way to measure productivity. Most professional usability tests involve at least ten subjects, but you can test with 95% certainty using as few as three. You can go through a months-long recruitment process, or you can call anyone with an intermediate experience level. You can test in a dedicated usability lab with a specialized observation room, or you can set up a computer in your office's conference room. You can write a 50-page deliverable that recommends a wholesale overhaul of a mostly completed product, or you can write a single page of suggestions for something that's still in the early stages of development. The economical alternatives to rigorous testing provide enough useful results that the significant added cost usually isn't worth it.

Steve Krug's *Don't Make Me Think* and *Rocket Surgery Made Easy* (New Riders Press) cover discount usability testing at length, including how to conduct a test and common issues you'll encounter.

PAPER PROTOTYPES.

Section 2.6 discussed the value of sketches as a fast and inexpensive brainstorming tool. Readable, clean sketches can be used as slapdash prototypes to test significant usability problems before any code is written.

Printing out graphical mockups or wireframes accomplishes the same thing, but takes more time.

Paper prototypes help test hierarchy, layout, and rudimentary behavior. They're especially useful for products with more structure and static content, like small to mid-sized websites.

To evaluate paper prototypes, you need someone to guide the test in addition to your test subject. The guide will swap out various prototypes as the user proceeds through various layouts. Often it's useful to mark out the monitor's area on the table with four strips of tape, to encourage the user not to move the prototype around. Then it proceeds like any other usability test: you have them perform a specified series of tasks. Time how long it takes, record any noteworthy successes or errors, and count how many steps it took to accomplish the task.

Unfortunately, paper prototypes haven't witnessed very much adoption. People think it's comical to do something so simple and cheap. If you think that applying usability testing to unrefined sketches is too reductive to be useful, it's worth remembering that the earlier you test for usability, the better the product's final state. Paper prototypes work best near the beginning of the design process, and would likely reveal major layout issues.

HEURISTIC EVALUATION.

Heuristics are metrics by which interfaces' simplicity, clarity, and usefulness can be evaluated. **Heuristic evaluation** is a kind of usability testing that figures out how a product best fulfills a series of heuristics, and then offers suggestions for how to solve any issues.

As with conventional usability testing, you can use heuristic evaluation to judge design effectiveness at any level of fidelity, from sketch to fully working product. The main difference is that heuristic evaluation tends to be conducted with expert users (or other designers) who are familiar with your product's heuristics. Expert users can evaluate an interface for small details, like performance hits or subtle rendering errors.

Between three and five people should evaluate the design, to get multiple opinions and a comprehensive analysis of the product. But if constraints prevent your testing with three people, testing with one person is still better than none.

Heuristic evaluation should be performed by those familiar with the craft, but this doesn't mean you need to spend thousands of dollars hiring a consultancy to do it. It's easy to train yourself and others, especially because there's a lot of latitude in what constitutes a good heuristic evaluation. Some characteristics are common to all good evaluations, though:

- Each evaluator should evaluate the product with the same set of heuristics.
- Each evaluator should review the product alone.
- Each evaluator should review the product at least twice. The first review is to analyze layout, context, and overall tone; the second is to analyze specific elements or behaviors.
- Reports can be organized in two different ways. Evaluators can list each heuristic and describe what parts of the interface do (or don't) fulfill each. Or they can organize it by element, and describe what heuristics do (or don't) apply to each.
- Each evaluator should write a report of their findings.

Write a summary of these reports, and use it to justify future design decisions.

Testing with more than five people will provide a negligible increase in useful data.

Beyond this, all it takes is practice. You can train many stakeholders to be evaluators if they know the product especially well, and it's easy to work with the people that you have.

Unless experts are your only target group – which is unlikely for the vast majority of products – heuristic evaluation should complement testing with intermediate users.

Fortunately, usability testing is usually easier, faster, and cheaper than heuristic evaluation, and it's more appropriate for checking products at every stage of their development. It ensures that major problems are fixed: layout, copy, or fitting the product's context.

Rapid iterations.

All of this functions best when you have a rapid, iterative development process. You start with something rough, and then build on it to create something that works well. Along the way, you question your own decisions through user testing and heuristic evaluation.

It also makes sense to test your product at early stages when you can iterate it repeatedly. Testing earlier beats testing later by such a magnitude that it makes no financial sense to forgo it. It helps refine your mission, and it gets user input into your project immediately. You can offer many solutions; testing allows you to choose the best ones and build upon those; *frequent* testing allows you to do this repeatedly.

These are necessary steps in a sound development process. They push you to make something better; they open your mind to alternate solutions; they allow you to second-guess your original plans and pivot quickly in response.

In software development, the best practice for rapidly iterating is called the **agile development model**, which favors frequent iterations and upgrades on a daily, weekly, or bi-weekly basis. Agile creates a workable, usable product as quickly as possible. It ensures that flaws are exposed and fixed early, and that new features can be developed and iterated in a similar fashion.

Embracing agile is a procedural and attitudinal shift away from the traditional model of conducting quality assurance and vetting against many stakeholders, called the **waterfall model**. Agile requires buy-in from all developers, or the process will slow down and become less effective.

Rapid iterations hinge on starting small and building the product carefully – which, of course, plays into notions of simplicity. Starting small is discussed in detail in 5.3.

For the data supporting this claim, check out Jakob Nielsen, "Paper Prototyping: Getting User Data Before You Code," Alertbox, http://www.useit.com/alertbox/20030414.html.

The agile development model has considerable support and widespread traction, but some good starting points include:

- · Mike Beedle et al., "Twelve Principles of Agile Software," The Agile Manifesto, http://www.agilemanifesto.org/principles.html .
- · Agile Alliance, http://www.agilealliance.com .
- · James Shore, *The Art of Agile Development* (O'Reilly Media), 2007.

4.1.12. *Understanding expectations is a never-ending process.*

Expectations age quickly and horribly. Figuring them out requires constant adaptation; technology changes too quickly for our desires to stay still.

Research is constant, and success is a pendulum; we struggle as we gain and lose ground. Find peace in this. Know that you'll never know everything. Search for joy in the attempt.

4.2. Manage the user's expectations.

Robert Pirsig, on a motorcycle fixed with an aluminum can:

I was seeing what the shim **meant.** *He was seeing what the shim* was. *That's how I arrived at that distinction. And when you see what the shim is, in this case, it's depressing. Who likes to think of a beautiful precision machine fixed with an old hunk of junk?*

Robert Pirsig, *Zen and the Art of Motorcycle Maintenance* (Bantam), 55.

4.2.1. Feedback should be helpful.

Feedback and instructions can help correct errors before they're made. Links can be added after form fields, directing the user to inline help. Or a paragraph of copy can precede a form with instructions. Or copy can be placed in a sidebar, for the user to follow as they enter information. And while form validation is ideal, adding "Entries should be in the form of…" blurbs is better than nothing.

Products should provide subtle but firm encouragement that errors are easy to overcome and working with the product remains feasible. Good products understand the shortcomings of users, and they address them before they pose problems. To users this comes off as clairvoyance, but to the designer it's simply a matter of being well-prepared.

4.2.2. Address common forms of error.

Nobody can design a perfect interface that accounts for every problem. When errors are made, the resulting feedback should be concise but descriptive, pointing users to the right answers without any technical jargon.

I mentioned Don Norman in 2.7 for coining the term "natural mapping." In *The Design of Everyday Things*, he also talks about the different categories of errors that users can make, categorized as slips and mistakes. **Slips** are errors that occur subconsciously, when we unthinkingly make errors in otherwise routine procedures. **Mistakes** are when you consciously misinterpret a product's basic function: you think it does one thing, but it does another instead.

Don Norman, *The Design of Everyday Things* (Doubleday Business), 106-7.

Norman discusses slips in much greater detail, but I'll summarize the different kinds here:

· *Capture errors* are when you perform one task frequently, and then you perform a slightly different task as if it were the frequent task. For example, one time I took the morning off work to go to a doctor's appointment. Rather than take the bus to the doctor's office, I woke up and took the train straight downtown to my workplace. But the process of waking up and getting ready resembled what I do before work every day, and so I interpreted the morning's events as requiring that I go to work.

Don Norman, *The Design of Everyday Things* (Doubleday Business), 107-8.

· *Description errors* are when you apply an action to a process that appears similar. Don Norman's example is helpful: "A person intended to put the lid on a sugar bowl, but instead put it on a coffee cup with the same size opening." Description errors tend to happen when two objects are near each other, like every time you press an adjacent key on a keyboard, flip the wrong switch in a long row of switches, or right-click when you mean to left-click.

· *Data-driven errors* occur when people perceive some sort of information and mean to communicate something different afterward, but instead recite the original information. For example, let's say I'm instant messaging a friend and they give me their new cell phone number. At the same time, I'm on the phone with the electric company, and they ask for my phone number. Instead, I provide my friend's.

· *Associative activation errors* are when you respond to similar stimuli identically. Another example from Norman: the phone rings, so you pick it up and say "Come in" as if the caller had knocked.

· *Loss-of-activation errors* are when you simply forget what it is that you were meant to do. You walk into your bedroom, for example, and wonder why you did so. You spend five minutes scratching your head, searching your room for objects you may have meant to pick up, until— ah-ha! You meant to turn the lights off.

For more information on modes – and why they cause more trouble than they're usually worth – see 6.5.

· *Mode errors* occur when you respond to a product that is in one mode as if it's in another, like entering a password when caps lock is accidentally enabled.

All of these errors can come up in your product, and your design should address as many of them as possible. You also have to account for the possibility that the user will completely misinterpret how to use your product: that a *mistake* will take place. Making elements and layouts as unambiguous and simple as possible helps to fix that.

4.2.3. Encourage undo.

Products need a way to account for error. The two most common methods are confirmation and undo. **Undo** reverses the action of the most recently completed step, while **confirmation** provides a second step before completing an action.

Confirmation requires an extra step every time a task is performed, but undo requires an extra step only when an error is committed. When scaled to every step of a product, enabling and encouraging undo can dramatically speed up a user's interaction. Confirmation prompts can usually be replaced with undo functions.

Undo works especially well when you can quickly backtrack across multiple steps. Undo histories can be recorded, to preserve entire paths. Undo history should also be preserved between openings of a file, or instances of a program, so it doesn't erase when you close the file or quit the program.

4.2.4. Streamline input.

Don't create a longer path when a shorter one will do.

Removing unnecessary screens.

Sometimes, entire layouts are excessive. Two separate pages can be combined, or one page can be removed entirely.

Many websites organize complicated inputs with multi-page forms; for instance, e-commerce sites will prompt for shipping information on one page and billing information on another. This is a fine line to walk. Sometimes it's sensible and appropriate to differentiate between similar types of input, because it reduces perceived complexity. But in time-sensitive situations, like purchasing tickets to a popular event, it can slow down the user and interrupt their flow. Make sure you can justify the trade-offs in adding pages this way.

Prominent navigation.

Google once boasted that they wanted users to spend as little time on their site as possible – because they could find the information that they wanted quickly and leave to explore the rest of the web.

Navigation should encourage that response by being prominent and unambiguous. Electronic book readers have prominent back and forward buttons, to shift through pages easily.

This claim peppers the Internet, but one such instance is from Paul Nelson, "Interview: Esteban Walther, Google head of travel Europe," Travel Weekly, http://www.travelweekly.co.uk/Articles/2007/02/08/23713/interview-esteban-walther-google-head-of-travel-europe-8-feb.html .

Newer word processors and spreadsheet applications have an all-in-one toolbar that controls most functions with a maximum of two steps. These are means of wayfinding, and the same principles apply to them.

Home → Culture → Careers

Contextually appropriate navigation.

Just as navigation should be prominent, it should also adapt to the section that you're on. It should mark your place, knowing where you've gone and how you arrived there.

If your navigation is a list of primary sections, then navigating to one should then provide a list of that section's sub-pages. If needed, a **breadcrumb trail** can show the path that someone took. On the web, breadcrumb trails show linked titles of each page in the site hierarchy, to show where they came from and how they can get back there. Users sometimes prefer breadcrumb trails to using the back button, especially when they enter a site through an external link.

This raises some interesting layout questions. Many layouts initially provide no room for sub-navigation. Simply adding it in a prominent place disrupts the layout, with a high risk of distraction. And hiding the subnav until needed risks the impression that nothing has changed.

It's possible to include subnav in every menu to begin with, but that doesn't scale to larger products and it won't convey where the user has just been. There are many potential solutions, but all of them pose trade-offs, and it's difficult to shift from one to another in a finished product.

Crud interfaces.

Crud stands for "create, read, update, delete," which are the four tasks that you should encourage whenever a product has to work with information. In short, *allow input wherever output exists.*

Never force users to conduct additional steps to transition from the add process to the edit process. They should be one and the same.

4.2.5. Remember the user's place.

Thoughtful products remember the user's actions; intelligent products learn the user's habits. When the user stops interacting with a product, it should save the last state. Reopening it should, by default, put the user back at that state, rather than some blank slate.

Ignore this rule if the user prompts a program with some sort of input, like if they want to open a file. The program should open the file, but preserve the saved state for the user to revert to if they so desire.

4.2.6. Never provide the ability to reset a form.

A reset button never does anything that refreshing the page, an undo function, or manually clearing the form fields can't also do. Inserting this button – often next to the submit button, which does the exact opposite thing – increases the chance of an error that would force re-entry. If it's absolutely necessary to backtrack so significantly, there are better ways to do it.

4.2.7. Controls should show the function, not the state.

When a control toggles between two states, it should convey that selecting it would trigger the intended behavior. For example, if you have two states for a control – on and off – and it's currently off, the control should read ON, so as to convey that triggering it will turn the thing on. Then, once it's triggered, it should turn on, and change to read OFF.

4.2.8. Work should be automatically saved, and saved work should be easily recalled.

Automatic saving preserves work and saves time. The product can periodically save time-stamped backups as the user works, while providing minimal, unobtrusive feedback each time one is saved. Scaled up, this can substitute for saving manually, spanning dozens of drafts, with no intrusion and relatively little disk capacity.

There should also be some way to recall backups, and to merge existing work with old copies. This could be integrated into the FILE menu of many editors as a RECOVER command, showing the list of timestamped versions and offering the opportunity to open them as if they were separate documents.

Automatic save and recovery should be turned on by default, unless the average document's file size is too large or disk space is prohibitive.

4.2.9. Monitor progress to fit the user, not the process.

Displayed progress is a natural mapping between an interaction and its feedback. While there are many different ways to accomplish this, progress bars are the most common. For computational tasks, progress bars should be a function of time taken. They can be weighed based on the results of previous tasks, which works towards better accuracy.

When progress doesn't naturally map to time taken, the interface lies to the user. Progress bars that jerk erratically towards their finish teach the user nothing about the process. It's endlessly frustrating when a progress bar hangs on some massive procedure at 99% for ten minutes. If you can't display an accurate progress bar, show different information.

Simultaneous progress bars.

Many tasks run simultaneously. Progress bars should be laid out such that these tasks can convey feedback at once, so the user can interpret overall progress. As a result, layouts need to afford the addition of more than one progress bar.

Highlighting completed tasks.

Showing a flat list of the computer's tasks is another way to imply progress on computations that have many discrete parts, especially in software installation or account creation. Then as tasks are completed, they can be highlighted in some way to indicate progress.

For example, as the computer works on a task, it can fade each list item from black text to some other color. As it *completes* each task, the type can switch from normal to bold. This offers a comforting, if imprecise, way of showing progress.

Estimates in copy.

Copy can offer an estimate based on your internet connection's speed, or your computer's processing power. From there, you can estimate the length of a task. This helps prepare the user to change their habits to fit the system's needs.

4.3. Elevate the user's expectations.

Author and actor Stephen Fry:

Don't you sometimes long to be CEO of a company like Sony Ericsson, Samsung, Nokia or Microsoft? So that you can say to your coders, your designers, your development teams and your software architects: "Not fucking good enough. I haven't said 'Wow' yet. I haven't gasped with pleasure, amusement or admiration once. Start again. Not fucking good enough."

Stephen Fry, "Gee, One Bold Storm coming up...", The New Adventures of Stephen Fry, http://www.stephenfry. com/2008/12/11/gee-one-bold-storm-coming-up/ .

4.3.1. Good interfaces bring technological progress.

Progress reframes the user's expectations, setting your product as the new standard. Progress makes the old seem uncool, boring, and frustrating. Progress is a display of courage.

When most companies make a successful product, their first impulse is to fiercely protect it and not make any substantial changes. But this is governed by fear. It's greedy and unsustainable. Standing still in the world of technology takes less effort, but it doesn't succeed in the long run.

If you pursue this, it won't be very long before someone else with more confidence than you makes the next great thing. Even when it looks like you're dominating the market, it can't hurt to drive down price and improve features to keep people's attention. Always keep making new things.

One solid perspective on how to change existing products comes from Marco Arment, "Side effects of developing for yourself," Marco.org, http://www.marco.org/392848093.

4.3.2. Provide wonder.

All the rigors of enforcing consistency and simplicity should blend into a clear vision for the way that a product should behave, giving it a personality all its own. Behavior becomes more than how a product responds to a stimulus: it allows us to predict other ways that it can work, without yet knowing how.

The joy that we get out of technology is put there by the designer. Good experiences make life memorable and beautiful. They provide a reason to go to work every day. They help us adopt constructive, enjoyable routines.

4.3.3. Create free interactions.

Sometimes it makes sense to add features that have no functional consequence, but nonetheless cause something perceptible to happen. They can subtly indicate a limit – like if a user selects something that's been disabled, or if they reach the

This passage is inspired by Chris Noessel, "One free interaction," Cooper Journal, http://www.cooper.com/journal/2009/01/one_free_interaction.html – which, in turn, is inspired by the "snapback" scrolling feature on iPhones.

end of a list. Free interactions always stay out of the way of the primary task; it should be entirely possible that a user never encounters one during daily use. Used well, though, they help define your product's personality.

No free interaction is essential for success. But they're easy to write, and they add tremendous value to a product's character. They're also good ways to indicate errors when users try to do something that they believed was valid.

Cadence:

5.1. Reorganize complexity.

Simplicity resists catering to edge cases, which are common in professional software. Advocating simplicity runs the risk of ignoring the uses that are important to a minority of people. Taken to extremes, advocating simplicity implies a judgment on people's habits, asking that they embrace software that doesn't do what they want.

When faced with necessary complexity, designers tend to either begrudge the fact, or embrace the challenge that it poses. I fall into the latter camp. It's a more optimistic perspective, it provides for consensus, and it frames complexity as something to work *with*, not against. Those of us with this latter perspective understand that complexity should still be useful and in line with the product's core functions.

Complexity is much more difficult to create and maintain than simplicity, and it should only be implemented when those additional features can't be removed. Some products can't be simplified any further without adversely affecting a significant number of users, so we need a way of dealing with complexity that respects its occasional necessity.

We gain a sense of accomplishment by solving many little tasks; conversely, we're often daunted when we face one enormous task. Finding ways to reorganize complexity can frame common problems, allowing us to begin solving them.

INCREMENTAL DISCLOSURE.

The most basic way to deal with complexity is by slowly revealing it across a series of steps.

On the web, using multiple pages for a form is a good method. When you have to collect a lot of essential information from new users, like on banking or e-commerce sites, it helps to segment form fields across multiple pages, an added benefit being that the users' progress can be saved and better tracked.

The initial screens of many products disclose essential features and copy. Subsequent screens incrementally reveal more information about the company or the product's function.

Drop-down menus and tabbed navigation also address the problem of a product's complexity by hiding its many additional functions until users need them.

And in the real world, we all know that the long lines for roller coasters are kept far out of public view and segmented so that they look like a series of short lines. Managing ex-

5:

Perceived accomplishment

pectations this way keeps ridership high, and people are less frustrated by a daunting wait.

GROUPING.

John Maeda summarized another way to deal with complexity on his personal blog:

John Maeda, "A... Ah ... Atchoo! Gestaltung!," Maeda's SIMPLICITY, http://web.archive. org/web/20080613184845/ http://weblogs.media.mit.edu/ SIMPLICITY/archives/000113.html

A complex system of many functions can be simplified by carefully grouping related functions.

With drop-down menus, extra functions are not only hidden, but grouped by related function. Eventually users figure out the conventions. For example, what's under the FILE menu in one application usually belongs under FILE in another.

In what other ways can related functions be grouped? Can patterns be used towards this end?

MODULARITY.

Modularity is the division of a large system into many smaller systems. Computer hardware is a classic example. The memory, processor, hard drives, or graphics card in many computers can be replaced with better components.

With software, third-party plugin technology extends the functionality of many applications, including photo editors, web browsers, and text editors.

In form design, especially complicated forms can be filled out in a modular way. Filing taxes online, for example, can be accomplished with whatever minimum of paperwork is essential to report - not every single form the government provides.

5.2. *Manage the user's locus of attention.*

Listening to music, one pays attention to the aspects of a song that are in the *perceived foreground*. A melody may stand out at one point, for instance, but after time a drum flourish may take its place. Skilled musicians know where their listeners' attention lies, how and when it changes, and how to manage it.

The same is true with interfaces. Users shift their attention from element to element as they interact with a product. In any situation, the **locus of attention** is the point where one is focusing at a given time. It can follow many paths, all with undefined outcomes. Potential paths create interference patterns with each other, making it hard to figure them out, yet still conditioning the user's mental processes. Attention is perception at its heart – and perception, combined with cognition, is the basis of interaction.

Each step presents two problems to the designer:

1. Identify where the user's locus of attention is.
2. Determine where and how to shift it in the next step.

Every visible element affects attention. You can mute certain elements and highlight others to establish a foreground relationship. You can alter their layout to imply a hierarchy. You can change the pliancy of elements to show which paths are feasible. Natural mappings can link labels to functions. Monotonous interfaces simplify the problem of locating a user's attention. Modeless feedback directs attention without distraction. Eliminating modes decreases the variance of paths, simplifying the interface and the diagnosis process.

In any interface, the quantity of paths increases exponentially with the number of unique ways to move from a given step. This directly correlates with the quantity of different places that a user's attention can be directed. Each pliant element that you add to an interface introduces a new potential path. From that path often comes a new layout and new elements – and, as a result, another series of paths. Systems become complex very quickly, and can be daunting if left unchecked.

For more on how path variance increases exponentially, see 2.2.

CONTEXT.

Context affects perception and attention as much as the interface itself. Understanding your product's context will help manage its users' attention. Where will it be used?

If you're making a mobile phone, for example, expect people to use it in all sorts of different lighting conditions, from near-total darkness to blinding sunlight. If you're building a desktop computer, you may design it to be less shock-proof or visible in direct sunlight than a laptop, enabling you to use higher-performance parts. If you're developing a mobile website for a large outdoor event, it should load very quickly, render clearly on a wide variety of devices, and anticipate a traffic spike during the event itself.

For more on platforms and systems determining your product's context, see 2.8.

POSTURE.

Posture, defined by Alan Cooper in *About Face*, describes how much of a user's attention a given product occupies on a platform or system.

Alan Cooper, *About Face* (Wiley), 127.

Some applications run best when maximized to the full screen, taking up all of your attention. Others run best as tiny icons in the menu bar, taking up almost no screen space. In between are windows of a variety of sizes, pliancy, and modality.

For example, the most currently popular music playing application almost always adopts a sovereign posture; it attempts to display a considerable amount of information about a list of songs, along with all the associated functions of playing and managing them, and entirely unrelated functions about cell phone applications, ebook management, and video playback. Their creators attempt to manage this with system-wide keyboard shortcuts for playback, as well as a special smaller mode that can better fit on a desktop; but these are admissions of the design flaws that have come from making one program perform too many core tasks.

Different postures affect the user's attention in different ways. If you're developing software, ask yourself: what posture does it have, and what impressions does it give users?

FEEDBACK.

The placement of feedback can drastically affect the user's flow. Some dialog prompts can render the rest of the interface inoperable until they're addressed. Others can stay to the side, away from the layout's primary elements.

2.3 discusses feedback at greater length.

Carefully consider the way that feedback directs attention. Take special note of instances where feedback occurs unexpectedly, or as the result of error.

5.3. *Start small and iterate slowly.*

START SMALL.

Chapter 1 discusses ground-up work on your product, and scaling slowly and carefully, at much greater length.

It's a romanticized notion, but most businesses really do begin out of someone's bedroom or garage. Small business owners can do quite a bit within the constraint of less money and resources - and these constraints give them a greater incentive to start making money.

Turning to music provides an appropriate sentiment. In the early eighties, a band called the Minutemen revolutionized punk rock under the idea that they "jam econo:" use few tools, record and tour on a stringent budget, and do most everything themselves. They wrote an influential, sprawling album - 45 songs in 81 minutes - that proved that skill and talent mattered more than tools or means.

Don't overshoot your abilities at the beginning. You start from an idea – hopefully a pretty good idea. Your tools affect, but don't necessarily limit, the beautiful and useful things that you can make.

ITERATE SLOWLY.

Andrew Burroughs, on iteration:

When things are designed, the most intuitive path or solution is usually the one that is chosen first. Over time, improvements are made... as a result, the design of an object often evolves away from that first intuitive idea. This results in interesting contrasts, especially when you see the "before" concepts and those that came afterward, side by side.

Andrew Burroughs and IDEO, *Everyday Engineering* (Chronicle Books), 41.

Build new things on what you already have. Evaluate the context of potential new features before implementing them, growing the product as a whole.

Avoid knee-jerk decisions when implementing new features. Deliberately make yourself wait too long before you begin to work on something new. If you're building with design patterns, focus on implementing one pattern at a time.

Don't build new features and fix bugs at the same time. Work should alternate between the two whenever possible, for they require very different procedures and mindsets. Only do both at the same time if the bugs are critical.

5.4. Build essential functions first.

If you're making a music player, it stands to reason that you should first build something that plays music well. Building the essential bit of a product provides its center: like the living room of a house, or a town square. With the center in place, you can create the functions which support that function: the rooms around the living room, the buildings around the town square, the buttons that control the player.

5.5. Know what your most fundamental tasks are.

Imagine that your product has only one function. What would that function be? The answer affects your company's mission and your product's goals, and helps build consensus and focus.

Word processors are good for writing documents. Music players are good for playing music. Email clients are good for reading and writing email. CD burners are good for burning CDs.

5.6. Don't mandate a specific format for information.

Information can take different forms in different areas of the world, and even from person to person. Fortunately, the variations are finite, and it's easy to account for most of them. Products should be smart enough to anticipate the possible variations in input, for *all* input.

A United States phone number entered into a form, for example, can take many different formats: 312-555-1212, 312.555.1212, 1-312-555-1212, +1 312 555 1212, (312) 555-1212, 3125551212, etc. All of these are valid phone numbers. Your product should work to accept them, rather than validate and enforce a single format.

Creative solutions exist for standardizing input. Entry can be validated and automatically completed on the fly, as a part of natural feedback. For example, if you're entering a telephone number into a form, your form can supply the bare essentials of a phone number, ( ) - , with the cursor after the opening parenthesis. As the user types *only numbers* into the form, it skips past the appropriate punctuation.

Entry that's validated on the fly is called **active validation** – as opposed to **passive validation**, which checks a given field once the user focuses away from it. In either situation, validation removes much of the risk of user error, as well as the need for server-side validation functions to handle input.

There are many different types of validation, from postal codes (some countries include letters in their postal codes; others do not) to states and provinces (e.g. Illinois v. IL). In all situations, though, you should trust that users know the proper way to enter information.

5.7. Require only essential information.

In every form, at least one field is required, otherwise you wouldn't have people fill it out in the first place. But which fields should you make required?

Form fields should only be required if they're essential to ensure passage from one step to the next. For example, one's email address and password should be all that's required to start an account on a website. Only ask for mailing addresses if you have to ship something, only ask for phone numbers if you have to call to validate a user's billing information, only ask for additional comments if they're essential to the form's purpose, and so on. If forms contain a mix of required and optional fields, required fields' labels should be suffixed with a * (e.g. PASSWORD *).

Finally, if users haven't filled out the required fields, any feedback that information is missing should be carefully worded, sympathetic, and unobtrusive. Ultimately it's *your* responsibility to ensure that people complete forms as you want; it's bad business to blame the user for those shortcomings.

5.8. Sort features into categories.

In 2.6, I discuss repurposable design patterns that can be used for organizing a layout's elements according to their purpose and function. Patterns apply to features as well. Features can be organized into a set of categories, which then determines layout and navigation:

1. **First**, *list all the features that you want to include,* how they will be visually expressed, what design patterns could affect them, and the way that they are supposed to behave. Label each with a number.
2. **Second**, *consider which features make the most sense together,* and group them accordingly.
3. **Third**, *prioritize each group* based on its relative importance to the product. You should designate only three to five priorities here – low, medium, and high will do.
4. **Fourth**, *name each group.* If you can't come up with a name for the group, reconsider its relevance to the product.
5. **Fifth**, *sketch each group.* Do this with whatever tools you'd like, but keep the process fast.
6. **Last**, *combine each of these features into a rough design.* Move the sketches around so the layout makes hierarchical sense.

This process doesn't need to occur separately from the one that's described in 2.6. Sketching features out is a good way to determine whether you've specified too many functions for them. Once you have a sense for how many features are just enough, then you can go through the rigorous process in 2.6 and figure out how specific elements work together.

5.9. Use preferences where they're appropriate.

Complex products often require preferences to customize the user's experience better. **Preferences** are modal controls that dictate more than one potential interface behavior.

People use products differently, and often the split between groups of common uses is more like $5\%_0$ than $9\%_0$. For these situations, and when it wouldn't make sense to build two separate products, preferences are the way to go.

Many platforms have consistent conventions for where preferences go. Since preferences are modal, they should go in the most conventional place that your context dictates, which is *always* out of the way of the rest of your product's functions.

Be less conservative with preferences around products that exclusively target experts, as they're used to tailoring their products to their own needs.

Preferences should roughly scale with the size of the product, and affect a subset of its features – not all of them.

5.9.1. *Take great care in determining defaults.*

Default preferences are a product's most common settings, making them the most important. Most users won't bother to reconfigure their products, and most novices won't even know that preferences exist at all.

For a long time, the most-hit website on the entire Internet was the default home page in Internet Explorer. Most passwords are among a list of only twenty common ones, like *password* or *123*. If the majority of your users will use your product in its default state, it makes no sense to make the product dependent on preference customization. Make sure the product, with its default settings, is the product done right.

5.9.2. *Preferences shouldn't interfere with use.*

Again, no product's operation should be contingent on its preferences. If people don't ever want to customize their product, they shouldn't have to. It should work fine out of the box.

5.9.3. *Preferences are features.*

Finally, preferences are subject to the same rules of simplicity as the rest of your product. Don't use them as an excuse for adding unnecessary features.

6.1. Products' cognitive cost should disappear after frequent use.

6:

Cognitive cost

Above any other concern, products should get out of the user's way. The best products become instinctual: we almost don't have to think about using them anymore. Our response to any product should become reflexive as soon as possible. Users already work towards this ideal, but they should succeed because of our designs, not despite them.

When using the web, users scan content as quickly as possible, remembering very little of any page. Users think in terms of their first impressions and don't take poor performance or crashing behavior as an excuse for good intentions.

We spend very little conscious effort on using technology, because we consider it a means to an end. Most of the time, we've already established expectations about how a product works. Once that happens, we try to get things done. So, typically we spend more time on accomplishing the task than learning the associated technology.

6.1.1. Common functions should be self-evident.

Your product's most essential features should be its most obvious. They should make your product's meaning evident to users of every experience level. Steve Krug said it best:

Making pages self-evident is like having good lighting in a store: it just makes everything seem better.

THE INVERTED PYRAMID RULE.

In 5.1, I discussed some ways to refactor complexity so that interfaces appear simpler. So which functions should you include on the starting screen?

Turning to journalism, the **inverted pyramid rule** has dominated reporting for most of its history, which says to organize an article's information from the most to the least important. Follow the inverted pyramid rule for your interface: make general tasks the most accessible, and specialized tasks the least.

For instance, an article from the New York times begins:

Barack Hussein Obama was elected the 44th president of the United States on Tuesday, sweeping away the last racial barrier in American politics with ease as the country chose him as its first black chief executive.

Douglas Hofstadter, *Gödel, Escher, Bach* (Basic Books), 26:

> No one knows where the borderline between non-intelligent behavior and intelligent behavior lies.

This point is corroborated at Aza Raskin, "Good Interfaces make Good Habits," http://www. azarask.in/blog/post/good-interfaces-create-good-habits/ .

Steve Krug, *Don't Make Me Think!* (New Riders Press), p. 19.

Adam Nagourney, "Obama Elected President as Racial Barrier Falls," New York Times, November 4, 2008. http:// www.nytimes.com/2008/11/05/ us/politics/05elect.html .

If you read *nothing else* in the article, you still know what happened. Someone was elected President of the United States on a Tuesday, his name is Barack Obama, he is the country's first black president. This paragraph is thick with details, but its main points are easy for any reader to understand.

If the reader is still interested, additional details are disclosed in descending order of importance. The article continues:

Mr. Obama, 47, a first-term senator from Illinois, defeated Senator John McCain of Arizona, 72, a former prisoner of war who was making his second bid for the presidency.

And then:

Not only did Mr. Obama capture the presidency, but he led his party to sharp gains in Congress. This puts Democrats in control of the House, the Senate and the White House for the first time since 1995, when Bill Clinton was in office.

Likewise with interfaces: essential tasks should be the most obvious. And the more niche the task, the more hidden it should be and the more effort it should take to reveal. Strata of complexity should cushion the user's exploration.

AFFORDANCES.

This quote is from Jane Fulton Suri and IDEO, *Thoughtless Acts?* (Chronicle), 170.

Affordances were first defined by James J. Gibson, *The Ecological Approach to Visual Perception* (Psychology Press). 2.9 provides more examples of affordances as they apply to human factors.

We perceive our environment "in terms of its possibilities of action," always asking what the world has for us. When a function is evident, its use is afforded as readily as possible.

In 4.1.1, I said that users perceive technologies as tools for accomplishing various tasks. The same may be said of affordances, which are only as good as our ability to take advantage of them. Employing affordances can solve many design problems.

For example:

- The shape of a door handle is a good example of an affordance; designed right, it conveys whether to push or pull.
- The supports of a bridge afford its proper function.
- The shape and weight of a manhole prevent its accidental movement, but its perforations allow water to drain through.
- The gears of a bicycle's drivetrain work with the chain and pedals to provide forward momentum.
- The woven structure of a chain link fence affords (and conveys) impermeability at a very low materials cost.

· The desire paths worn in grass fields from continuous foot traffic show the most common (if unsanctioned) way to get between two common points, and provide an opportunity to design a sidewalk.

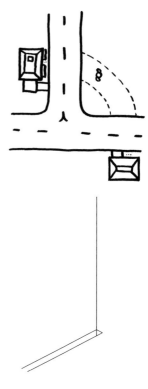

If a feature is going to afford its use, it has to imply its existence and behavior. It should be directly in the user's locus of attention. It also has to imply how to use it, and how it will behave.

The task of implying so much can be less daunting than it initially appears. In *Designing Design*, Kenya Hara alludes to a narrow rectangular groove cut in the floor along a house's foyer wall. Visitors rested their umbrellas inside the groove, leaning against the wall. The groove was not a conventional umbrella rack, but it afforded the exact same functions that a conventional rack would. As a rack, it was functionally complete because people used it unthinkingly and effortlessly.

Fitts' Law helps with the affordances of various on-screen elements. It posits that the time required to move to a given target on a computer screen is a function of the distance to that target. In modern interfaces, however, the edges and corners of a screen afford an *infinite-sized target* – because no matter how far your cursor moves, it remains at that point on the edge. Thus, the corners are the most important real estate on any graphical display that's operated by a mouse, and the edges are the second most important. For this reason, many crucial functions of an operating system are placed in these areas.

Fitts' Law is also a function of the dimensions of your target. For example, short, wide buttons are harder to hit if your cursor starts from a point directly above or below that button; while the button's area may be large, it's too short to move to reliably.

There are other ways to help afford use: emphasizing elements' pliancy, increasing their size, changing their color, and moving them closer to the center (in the user's way), the edges (to take advantage of Fitts' Law), or the left side (on the web, to take advantage of users' typical "F-shaped" reading pattern). In what other ways can you design a product's critical functions so they're easier to use?

6.1.2. *Paths should be self-evident.*

A product operates according to a set of rules, and those rules can be obvious or obtuse. When you open a product for the first time, the finite number of things that you can do with it provides a framework for further use. For each of these first steps, there's a set of second steps that you can take.

Kenya Hara, *Designing Design* (Lars Müller Publishers), 44.

A great summary of Fitts' Law is available at Kevin Hale, "Visualizing Fitts's Law," Particletree, http://particletree.com/features/visualizing-fittss-law/ .

Jakob Nielsen, "F-Shaped Pattern for Reading Web Content," Alertbox, http://www.useit.com/alertbox/reading_pattern.html .

The thinking behind this is indebted to Don Norman, *The Design of Everyday Things* (Doubleday Business), 119.

As alluded to in 2.2, paths branch out with exponential complexity per step. The entire set of paths and steps that a user could potentially take is called a **decision tree**.

Decision trees can be *wide* or *narrow*, meaning they can have many or few unique potential paths, respectively. They are also either *deep* or *shallow* – meaning once you start a path, it either takes many steps to complete a task, or few.

The best decision trees are narrow and shallow. They're easier to implement and simpler to think through.

Ostensibly simple decision trees are still surprisingly large. For example, tic-tac-toe has an extremely simple set of rules, learnable in only a few minutes. The decision tree for a tic-tac-toe game, expressing all unique types of moves by X and O, depicts eleven separate paths with a maximum of seven moves. When considering permutations of tic-tac-toe games, though, which account for unique squares and not the symmetry of a 3×3 board, there are over *fifteen thousand* different potential moves. But that's a drop in the ocean when compared to a chess board: its decision tree comprises approximately 10^{120} unique games. To put that in perspective, the observable universe contains approximately 1.5×10^{82} atoms.

There are only three kinds of first moves that you can make in tic-tac-toe: a corner, a side, or the center. Now think about all the ways that users can trigger behavior in the first screen of your product. Is it obvious where they should go first? Is your decision tree so wide that users may be confused about what to do next? Is it so deep that you'll lose them midway through the process?

Apply this process to subsequent steps. Each step possesses its own decision tree. Is this step contingent on feedback from previous steps? What are the user's expectations here?

Inherent to our intelligence is our ability to step back from the present task and suss out patterns in anything that looks like it could be systematic. It's how we're able to figure out something as complicated as a chess game. It's also what we mean, more or less, when we say we're figuring things out, and the most successful products reduce this process to a minimum.

6.1.3. *An interaction should proceed as quickly as the user's ability to process it.*

Gordon Moore, "Cramming more components onto integrated circuits," *Electronics* 38.8 (1965).

Moore's Law states that processor speeds double every two years. But the response time of computers hasn't increased accordingly, because we keep writing software that takes advantage of the extra processing power. Only recently have we worked to optimize what software we currently have, rather than writing more computationally demanding features.

The more demanding that we make software, the harder it is for us to optimize so it fits the speed of our own cognition. Users pay dearly for this: the cognitive cost of slower products affects their ability to work with the entire system.

People shouldn't feel limited by their technology – and they process information very quickly. The period between any two steps should be of negligible length, not more than 100 milliseconds. Interruptions in our cognition slow us down considerably, and response time forms our expectations for future performance.

But if we write yesterday's software to work on today's hardware, it runs much faster. I don't mean "yesterday's" in terms of features, or how social it is, or how many things it does, or anything like that. I mean how miserly it is in its resource use. I mean how much it tries to do, and what it elects *not* to do. Maybe if we code in this way, we won't write products that collapse under their own weight, either.

6.1.4. *Support the user's muscle memory.*

Muscle memory is the way that the human body trains its motor skills. As we grow up, we practice basic muscle memory: chewing, walking, speaking, climbing stairs. We develop these skills over time, and eventually stop thinking about them.

It's very hard to break people of a habit that's been committed to muscle memory. It's great when people know how to do things right, but when an inefficient way to complete a task is committed to muscle memory, it requires considerable effort to break the habit before anything new can be learned.

Our motor skills come in two categories: *fine* and *gross*. Fine motor skills concern small, precise actions, like typing, brushing teeth, writing, or eating. Gross motor skills require more substantial body movement: running, throwing, kicking, swinging a bat or racquet. Using small devices like a keyboard or mouse requires significant, repeated use of fine motor skills. We have to understand fine motor skills if we're going to understand how to put muscle memory to work in our products.

Fine muscle memory takes different forms, and is practiced to varying degrees. For example, if you haven't written for a long time, picking up a pen and trying to write for a long time often results in cramps and poor handwriting. The same goes for typing or mousing; it stands to reason that expert users have fewer problems using a keyboard and mouse than novices.

Robert Bringhurst, *The Elements of Typographic Style* (Hartley & Marks Publishers), 193:

> And we read the screen the way we read the sky: in quick sweeps, guessing at the weather from the changing shapes of clouds, or like astronomers, in magnified small bits, examining details.

The 100 milliseconds justification comes, in part, from Jakob Nielsen, "Response Times: the 3 Important Limits," *Usability Engineering*. Quoted in part at http://www.useit.com/papers/responsetime.html .

All of this plays into optimizing software for better performance. 1.6 elaborates on this at greater length.

A personal anecdote: I type with every finger on my left hand, but on my right hand, I type entirely with my pointer finger. That's how I learned how to type, and I doubt I'll ever be able to change it.

Keyboards, mice, touchscreens, and cell phone keyboards are all different to use, requiring different groups of muscles. All of these input methods are widespread now, practiced consistently by billions of people. And to confound the problem further, switching rapidly between two different input methods (the most common being keyboard and mouse) involves largely separate groups of muscles.

For a synopsis of input methods, take a look at John Gruber, "Where Keyboard Shortcuts Win," Daring Fireball, http://daringfireball.net/2008/01/where_keyboard_shortcuts_win .

Considerable research favors restricting the amount of input methods to only one. In the personal computer's case, this is the keyboard, since it involves less range of muscular movement. Keyboard-only interfaces are nearly exclusive to experts, though, since they usually require memorizing a series of complicated and product-exclusive shortcuts to perform basic tasks.

This means that cell phones with touchscreen input and software-based keyboards prosper from having only one interaction model for users to train on. It takes less short-term effort to learn, and less long-term effort to switch between physical and touch-based interactions.

REPETITIVE STRESS INJURIES.

All experience levels can suffer from repetitive stress problems, but – for obvious reasons – experts are at greatest risk.

Repetitive stress becomes an issue when anyone uses a product for an extended period of time. Practicing good ergonomics is the best solution, and that's the user's responsibility. But products have responsibilities of their own, and they can meet users partway.

By offering keyboard shortcuts, shorter paths, and encouraging repetitions that are less complex and require less strain (such as key combinations that are near each other on a conventional QWERTY keyboard), we can reduce the risk of repetitive stress injuries. On the hardware side, we can build narrower keyboards, more comfortable key layouts, touchscreens, and interaction models that require only one input method.

6.2. *Manage the user's workflow.*

Workflow models are a way to describe steps and paths. Usually expressed as a flow chart or numbered outline, they're useful for auditing paths to determine where to eliminate steps. They should address a task's intended goal, the relative frequency of each path, and if any actions are dependent on other actions.

Workflow models can be tied to usability testing by determining where the user's locus of attention should be at each step. This provides a good perspective for asking users what they're thinking, and seeing if it matches your expectations.

6.3. Create a rhythm of rapid, brief, and repetitive interactions.

Flow is the name of a psychological state, coined by Mihály Csíkszentmihályi in an influential book of the same name, that refers to the single-minded, deeply focused immersion of someone when performing a given task. Flow happens in countless skills. Csíkszentmihályi cites examples of musicians getting "in the groove" and athletes after considerable practice. Game developers have attempted to leverage flow's principles in order to make their games more engrossing.

Mihály Csíkszentmihályi, *Flow* (Harper Perennial).

Encouraging users' flow is a huge aspiration among interaction designers. Chances are you've experienced this state on any project where you stayed up late, deeply involved in solving a complex problem. It takes time and effort to experience flow, but it can be extremely satisfying and fulfilling. The most successful designs appear to provoke it effortlessly.

Once someone begins to work instinctively with any product, they become fluent in its slang: their intent is connected with the product's result. Conversely, people won't experience flow if your product is too idiosyncratic – and they'll think more highly of products that they can learn easily, that get out of the way of what they want to do.

One of the best ways to encourage flow is by providing a way to repeat similar tasks efficiently, leading the user to adopt a **rhythm**. A single iteration of a rhythm may appear inconsequential, but a larger purpose reveals itself when repeated many times. IDEO designer Andrew Burroughs acknowledge this:

A process's singular actions often appear to have no effect, but when they are repeated over and over again, there is a noticeable cumulative result. Such traces can reveal trends or interesting phenomena that otherwise might not be visible.

Andrew Burroughs and IDEO, *Everyday Engineering* (Chronicle Books), 135.

No matter what form it takes, rhythm has a fragile entropy: it's much easier to stop a rhythm than it is to create one. But we have a tendency to find regularity in any interface, if it's there for us to see. And repetition can happen with *any* element.

Rhythm or no, though, flow happens out of habit. Once we work with a product for long enough, its use is imprinted in our memory, framing how we handle future interactions. The main issue is how much effort it takes to experience flow, and what barriers we can remove to make it easier and faster.

Paul Rand, *A Designer's Art* (Yale University Press), 87:

The emotional force generated by the repetition of words or pictures ... should not be minimized.

For more on flow and memory, check out Jack Cheng, "Habit Fields," A List Apart, http://www.alistapart.com/articles/habit-fields/ .

6.3.1. Encourage the user to invent their own rhythms.

Rhythms are formed when the user unthinkingly repeats any brief action. Early instances of a repeated action affect the user's attitudes towards future instances. Well-designed products form a positive feedback loop that amplifies output, decreases a repetition's completion time, and can perpetuate indefinitely.

Rhythm helps shape our expectations; we start to expect repetitions after we've been trained to understand them. Once repetition is encouraged, the user will follow. Keyboard shortcuts, inline help, visual cues, and keyboard- or mouse-only applications all help to encourage rhythms.

For years, experts have finely tuned their workflows with keyboard shortcuts and fine-grained preference customization, adopting more complex rhythms than less experienced users.

6.3.2. It should take only one step to shift between two of a rhythm's repetitions.

This rule speaks for itself, but examples reinforce it.

Consider switching between successive form fields, moving between rows or columns of a spreadsheet, or switching between a PC's currently running applications. All of these require only one step, which makes it as easy as possible to adopt a rhythm.

See 6.5 for more information on modes.

Conversely, shifting between applications on many smartphones requires two steps: going to the home screen (or opening a list of recent apps), then selecting a new app. This excess step is ripe for reconsideration.

6.3.3. Compose elements with a visual rhythm.

The best way to enforce a readable layout is by placing elements such that the user can guess their locations. If two elements are placed five pixels apart, maybe the third should be placed five pixels apart from the second as well. This subconsciously trains the user to scan the layout in a consistent increment.

Towards that end, a **grid** is a consistent vertical or horizontal division of a layout, comprised of a column width, margin width, and number of columns. A **typographic baseline** is a specific line height for enforcing the placement of content across columns of a grid.

Most software and web layouts use grids of flexible height and a typographic baseline instead of a fixed number of rows. That said, try to enforce a horizontal grid and a fixed height when possible – and make the width : height ratio a precise value (such as 2 : 1, 16 : 9, or the golden ratio φ : 1).

Grids are the best way to bring visual rhythm to any layout. They establish the priorities of various elements, conveying them faster and more clearly, because they are arranged in a systematic, structured way.

Elements can span one or more columns of a grid, but they should be left- or right-aligned to a given column; centering an element risks appearing visually erratic. Here's a four column grid with generous margins, 1/4 the width of each column:

Most designers use translucent overlays to indicate grids when they're designing or wireframing on a computer. When I sketch grids, I use a thick, subtly off-white marker to indicate the margins. That way I can snap elements to the grid without distraction. That said, any color should do; pick what works.

While the possibilities are endless, grids come in a few traditional flavors. Choose the right grid based on what elements you have to organize. For example, a web page with five primary navigation elements would prosper with a five-column grid. If you need more than five columns, subdivide each column to yield ten or twenty. Some common grid divisions include 3/6/12 columns, 4/8/16 columns, or 5/10/20 columns. Grids beyond 20 columns lose their effectiveness because it's harder to differentiate between adjacent columns as a layout is scanned. And fine-grained subdivisions should be used sparingly; the best grids are simple grids, numbering 6 columns or fewer.

Cadence & Slang's body columns are in 8pt text with an 11pt baseline. The sidebar columns are 8pt text with a 9pt baseline.

A good baseline is around 120% to 140% of your body text's font size. All elements should be aligned to the baseline.

We can impose a baseline upon our previous grid:

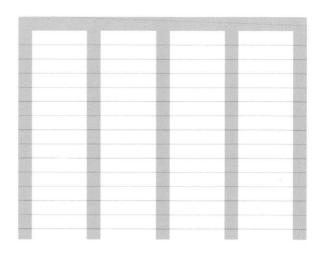

The layout has only one baseline, which makes the text in one column line up with the text in another. Adding some sample content helps convey this:

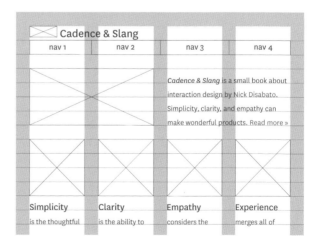

Not only do the text blocks fit the baseline, but images have been sized to be a consistent multiple of the baseline as well.

Larger text can fit a taller baseline, or be doubled in size to fit a shorter one. Short baselines are well-suited to long blocks of text, and tall baselines are better for headline- and image-heavy layouts. In either case, though, the baseline height should be consistent across the product.

THE BENEFITS OF GRIDS.

For years, print designers have used grids and baselines to make text more readable and layouts more scannable. The techniques pioneered in the mid-twentieth century are directly applicable to laying out interfaces, and they're crucial to ease of use.

Josef Müller-Brockmann comments thus:

The use of the grid as an ordering system is the expression of a certain mental attitude inasmuch as it shows that the designer conceives his work in terms that are constructive and oriented to the future.

And:

The systematic presentation of facts, of sequences of events, and of solutions to problems should, for social and educational reasons, be a constructive contribution to the cultural state of society and an expression of our sense of responsibility.

Grids make elements easier to organize and text easier to read. They impose a light, qualified rigor on the entire product.

Grids are the positive consequence of good engineering. They imply a familiarity, a confidence. They form the rhythm of your layout – to know that if one element is *here*, it stands to reason that the next element will be *there*. And while they're not essential for good interactions (nor is a tempo essential for beautiful music), they certainly help.

Some designers believe that grids are too constraining, that they stifle creativity. But they're a good frame for creative solutions, and too subtle a constraint to affect most design negatively. Grids form the tempo of your layout; they dictate the sensible placement of elements and do a sizable amount of work for you.

Plus, if you find your current grid confining, you can always come up with another grid.

Because interfaces link so strongly with users' expectations, you can't afford to ignore the constraints of a grid. They can be imposed on *any* interface. The benefits of a solid grid and

On the web, many frameworks exist to enforce grid divisions and a baseline: plug in the values that you want, and a script calculates the corresponding stylesheet. Blueprint, located at http://blueprintcss.org, is an early, influential framework.

Josef Müller-Brockmann, *Raster Systeme Fur Die Visuele Gestaltung* (Niggli), 10.

Ibid., 12.

1.9 has more on the benefit of constraints.

baseline far outweigh the risks afforded by not using them, and this rule should only be broken if you're absolutely sure how and why you're doing so.

6.4. *Express quantitative information densely.*

Quantitative information can be displayed in countless forms. The most common ones are graphs and maps, but DNA, train schedules, football plays, and countless other uses have taken radically different, singular forms.

In his book *Envisioning Information*, Edward Tufte proposes the axiom *to clarify, add detail*. The average human eye can distinguish between extremely small distances, far more than most displays give us credit for. Many graphs – especially bar and line plots – offer only a few points of information, but it's been proven (especially by Tufte, in *The Visual Display of Quantitative Information*) that we're capable of understanding so much more, in about as much time as it takes to understand a USA TODAY infographic.

According to Tufte, information display should enforce comparisons between nearby values, show multiple variables in two-dimensional space, and integrate text with images and data. **Information density** – how many data points are expressed in a given area – is important towards these goals, but it becomes especially crucial in an interface. Technology has a tremendous opportunity to display large data sets creatively, so users may understand the powerful narratives that they imply.

Most current platforms pose challenges to dense information. The human eye can see at about 3,000 DPI (distinctions per inch), but the average computer screen remains, as of press time, 110 DPI. Smartphones currently run between around 130 and 320 DPI. Current electronic book readers are around 170 DPI.

Well-made print media continues to have a huge advantage over electronic media when it comes to dense narrative-based information display. But this constraint, while enormous, doesn't prevent these sorts of display from happening. People have implemented creative solutions in the past, from zooming in on visually complicated images to providing tab-based navigation that overlays a given map or graph.

6.4.1. *Use sparklines to provide lightweight, contextual information display.*

As mentioned in 2.8.3, **sparklines** were invented by Edward Tufte as a way to describe short time-series of data in a narrow,

Edward Tufte, *Envisioning Information* (Graphics Press), 88-89.

The first 72 DPI displays were mass-markted fifteen years before this book's publication. *Cadence & Slang* is printed at approximately 2,400 DPI.

Kenya Hara, Designing Design (Lars Muller), 146 states that before the insurgency of digital graphic design, Japanese printmakers and artists were trained to draw ten distinct lines between two lines a millimeter apart. Now you can do that on a computer in ten minutes.

word-length space. For example, here's a sparkline of the 97-64 win-loss record of the Chicago Cubs in 2008, where up denotes a win, a horizontal underline indicates a home game, and a red tick means the game was won or lost by two or more runs:

When shrunk to the right proportions, this information is dense enough to describe a set of games with as much meaning as an essay on the subject. Notice the winning streak about two-fifths of the way through, and the textbook fall slump in the last fourth of the season. With other teams' win-loss records, readers can also determine whether the Cubs made the playoffs. Depending on one's fan loyalties, this affects different people in different ways, and the presentation gets out of the way to tell the story that these different people want to hear.

Sparkline created from Bryan Donovan, "Custom MLB Team Sparklines", Hardball Times, http://www.hardballtimes.com/thtstats/main/sparklines/custom.php.

6.4.2. *Give graphs context and truth.*

Information shouldn't lie. Make sure your axes are accurate. Don't put breaks in your axes like —//— unless you absolutely have to. Make sure the scale of your x-axis is the same as your y-axis when you're comparing two of the same unit (time, distance, weight, etc).

It stretches the truth to blow scales out of proportion. Tufte defines the **lie factor** of a data display as the size of effect shown in a graphic, divided by the size of that same effect in the data. Ideally, the lie factor should be 1.0, showing a 1:1 mapping between perceived magnitude and data increase. In *The Visual Display of Quantitative Information*, he shows a graph with a lie factor of 59.4, showing a size increase of 27,000 percent to express a data increase of 454 percent. Keep your graphs' lie factor at 1.0, and don't add anything to an information display that distracts your audience from understanding the data.

For more on non-data ink that doesn't contribute to the information's narrative, or "chartjunk," check out 3.7.

6.5. *Avoid modes.*

In 2.2, I defined a **mode** as "any kind of setting that a user can trigger to activate a different set of behaviors on an otherwise identical interface." The caps lock key is an obvious kind of mode, but modes can exist in software, too. A mode is one of multiple (usually two) states; a **state** is a behavior (or set of behaviors) that occurs when triggering an element that is affected by changes in the mode.

In his book *The Humane Interface*, Jef Raskin formally defines an interface as:

Jef Raskin, *The Humane Interface* (Addison-Wesley Professional), 42.

modal with respect to a given gesture when (1) the current state of
the interface is not the user's locus of attention and (2) the interface
will execute one among several different possible responses to the
gesture, depending on the system's current state.

Dialog boxes don't have to be modal, but if they disable the rest of the layout until action is taken, they are.

Alan Cooper, *About Face*, p. 430:

A dialog box is another room; have a good reason to go there.

4.2.2 has more on mode errors.

Any lightbox or dialog box – one that disables the rest of a product until it's acted upon – is a mode. Toggling italic text on and off in a word processor is a mode. Changing tools in a photo editing program: each tool is itself a mode.

By definition, a mode's state is outside the user's locus of attention, which flouts their expectations and leads to errors. Modes that disable the rest of a layout artificially restrict the paths that a user can take, pointing to issues with the code (it can't do the dirty work of handling different inputs) or layout (it isn't naturally conducive to the most common modes).

Modes are harbingers of design flaws. Ideal products are modeless, and modes should be eliminated whenever possible. Modes have been viewed as a necessary evil in our field for decades, but they've become increasingly hard to justify when we now have so many ways to eliminate them.

6.5.1. Feedback should be modeless.

Feedback is modeless when it's built into the layout. Modeless feedback doesn't interrupt the user's current process, and it's well-suited to show any sort of status. In any case where you can replace modal feedback with modeless feedback, do so.

This may be slower going than I let on here. For more on the sad state of display resolutions, see 6.4.

As displays support higher resolutions, more feedback can be executed modelessly. Icons can convey more than just the file type: half-downloaded files from a web browser, for instance, can have their preview icons replaced with a progress bar. Hover states and marginal text can convey data as a user hovers over different parts of a map or data table.

One good example of modeless feedback is the character count and line number in plaintext editors: it exists inline, without having to pull up a separate word count dialog. And on the web, form confirmation can be executed with inline copy, rather than a modal alert to show success or failure.

The trade-off is that modeless feedback adds elements to a user's display – this can be distracting, especially for novices, when taken to extremes. Be careful about what kind of feedback you choose to add, and how and when it appears.

6.5.2. Don't disable the layout with any dialog prompt.

One of the most common ways to prompt another step is with a dialog prompt – either asking for preferences, or the infamous "Are you sure? OK/CANCEL". But disabling the layout with any dialog prompt or modal overlay requires excess effort to figure out the new mode.

Ideally, dialogs should be placed in the layout. If dialog prompts must be used, the rest of the layout should be pliant, and it should be possible to move the overlay out of the way to conduct other tasks.

6.5.3. Remove modal dialogs through layout changes.

By moving elements around and approaching behavior differently, you can keep once-modal displays out of the way and allow greater freedom of input.

Here are some easy ways to remove modes through layout. In all of these cases, modeless dialogs should be applied with consistent appearances and behaviors.

A SECOND COLUMN.

Consider a two-column layout: your primary layout on one side, and feedback on the other. This sort of layout makes feedback dependent on the user's primary input, which could mean that it would have to change after every step. Two-column layouts like this are more usable, but likely take more work to program.

EXPANDING THE LAYOUT.

Consider expanding the layout to fit new prompts when they're needed. A group of elements could move out of the way to fit a given prompt, or white space could exist preemptively. Both ways provide enough room to place feedback, with many possibilities for conveying meaning without distraction.

DRAGGABLE POP-UPS.

Consider popups that appear over the layout without disabling it. These popups could potentially be draggable, to move out of the way; but then many popups could accumulate without any action on them. Only use these if they fit the function and layout more appropriately than any alternative.

A good methodology for designing without modes on the web: Aza Raskin, "Designing without Modal Overlays," http://www.azarask.in/blog/post/designing-without-modal-overlays/ .

37signals also touches on this at Ryan Singer, "Modal Overlays Beyond the Dialog Box," Signal vs. Noise, http://www.37signals.com/svn/posts/1149-modal-overlays-beyond-the-dialog-box .

One noteworthy constraint, however: the smaller the screen, the less freedom you have to move elements. So the smaller your screen, the harder modes become to eliminate.

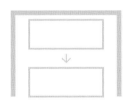

CREATIVE SOLUTIONS.

Layout has infinite possibilities. If the solutions listed here don't work, then something else will. Be creative in finding layout solutions. Surely new possibilities will reveal themselves as new platforms and systems are released, with novel interaction models that this book could never foresee.

6.5.4. *Replace modes with quasimodes.*

Quasimodes are modes that require conscious user input to activate and deactivate. Returning to the caps lock analogy: caps lock is a mode, while holding down the shift key is a quasimode. Click-dragging to select multiple items is a quasimode; so is holding down the shift key and clicking on several items. Drop-down menus are a quasimode. Quasimodes are generally hard to find, but easy to learn once found.

Quasimodes benefit the user because they eliminate the possibility of mode errors. At the same time, quasimodes are constrained because they can generally be used only to control your system, not to input information. The shift key is a quasimode because it changes your keyboard into a different character set, but it doesn't actually type any letters for you. Quasimodes also involve a higher cognitive cost, because the user has to think about when to turn them on or off.

Most users know what quasimodes are, even if they may not call them by that name. They're very powerful for improving your product's functionality, with little development cost and far reduced risk of user error. How can quasimodes replace modes for those who are willing to learn them?

Different cultures form design slangs that speak well to some people and alienate others. At the same time, certain designs try to appeal to many people, across cultural and age boundaries.

Your design can speak to as few or as many people as needed. Each approach has its trade-offs. The fewer people you target, the more intimately you can communicate with them, and the more likely that you can pare down many features. The more people you target, the more potential business you have, but risking trade-offs and potential dissatisfaction in the product.

Each extreme may be undesirable. It doesn't make sense to write products that are so overly styled that they target only a few people, and it rarely makes sense to write something that pleases the whole human race. There's a middle ground that amasses and preserves customers.

7:
Cultural norms

7.1. Account for the plurality of cultural manners.

Different cultures ascribe different meanings to various symbols. All icons and nomenclature should be vetted for translation into other languages and deployment in other countries. For example, in most parts of the Middle East, the thumbs up hand 👍 means roughly the same as the United States' middle finger. Would you want *that* for your OK button?

This also applies to products written for your home country. The common way to force a program to close on Linux or BSD is by typing "kill" – not exactly the nicest option, especially when synonyms like close, quit, or end exist.

7.2. Account for the plurality of religious customs.

Imagery that's innocuous in one country may be offensive or suggestive in another. For example, the Red Cross is called the Red Crescent in Islamic countries because of the religious connotations of a cross. And more infamously, the swastika symbol is used in many Eastern religions, but its association with the Third Reich and Nazism tainted its meaning in much of the world.

When using any sort of symbols or iconography, make sure they're vetted to ensure a consistent meaning across cultures. Fortunately, there are quite a few easy solutions online. Offline, Carl G. Liungman's *Dictionary of Symbols* (Norton Paperbacks) is a good source for tracing the history and context of icons.

7.3. Account for the plurality of non-Latin scripts and reading direction.

Hello, world.

שלום

While it may be translated into other languages someday, this book is written in English, which reads left to right, top to bottom. Other scripts across the world have different reading directions, which affects the way that native readers perceive any layout, printed or electronic.

This affects the way that text is displayed, of course, but it also affects layout. Some major websites reverse the left-right orientation of their layouts for Hebrew or Arabic readers. For example, Arabic sites put their navigation on the right sidebar. For products developed in Latin languages, navigation should be put on the left sidebar, as users rarely read content on the right side of a page.

Thousands of scripts have their own conventions, and alphabets that may seem identical to English have their own quirks. For example, German and French have ß and Œ, Vietnamese has a vast and complex set of diacritics, and Hungarian hyphenates the common word *össze* as *ösz-sze*.

"össze" is a prefix for "together".

Is your product sensitive to these concerns? Products native to their home countries likely are, giving them an advantage over yours. If you're developing a product in San Francisco that you want people to use in Thailand, then you should work to make it familiar and inviting to that culture.

7.4. Define the tone of the design based on your target culture.

Molly E. Holzschlag, "Putting the World into 'World Wide Web'," 24 Ways to Impress Your Friends, http://24ways.org/2005/putting-the-world-into-world-wide-web.

A regional vernacular is taking shape, as users gravitate around social networks and instant messaging services that address the needs attendant to their cultures. Within specific cultures, different economic classes and experience levels are more likely to sign up for certain services than others.

This is a controversial point – that poor people use one product and rich people another, or young one and old another, or novices one and experts another – but enough data has been amassed over the past decade to corroborate it. It's an open question whether products should attempt to cater to multiple (or all) segments, or whether it makes more sense to build products that target just one. Frequently, products target just one demographic, broaden to others, and then collapse under the weight of being everything to everyone. Products commonly fail when ported to new countries.

If we apply the rest of this book consistently – that simplicity is better, and that products that do less and target narrow groups of people are more useful – then it stands to reason that products should be written for narrow demographics. But taken to an extreme, this can isolate people, and keep them from understanding each other. We already speak of "walled gardens" between social networks; as technology becomes more prevalent, these walls extend into our personal relationships.

But one real-life example gives me hope. Here in Chicago, everybody uses the subway. The rail line that I ride to work every day is full of a diverse range of people – all the more surprising in a famously segregated city. And yet we're all using the same thing to get around, because it's designed to be convenient, affordable, and demographically neutral. It's a success by that measure, and it gives me hope that we too can create things that appeal to many different people.

7.5. Neutralize the product if different demographics will use it.

We can potentially find demographic consensus by neutralizing a product: using indistinctive colors, spare graphics, and traditional typefaces. Products with neutral design adjust more easily to a variety of people.

Simplicity could be the answer here, when it's executed with the intent to bring others into the fold. By adopting a more neutral voice and paring down any visual cues that could imply cultural connotation, many products could speak to a wider range of people – and people could more easily project their values, aesthetics, and ideas onto the product.

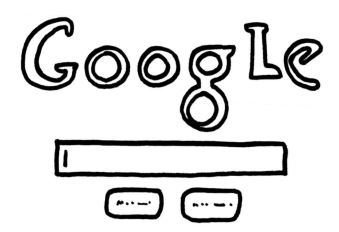

7.6. Release separate products if cultural differences are mutually exclusive.

Translating a product into a new language is a much easier proposition than changing the product's conventions to best reflect a demographic's social customs. But this is frequently necessary, to ensure familiarity and empathy towards its audience.

When deciding how to change a product's interface for different demographics, inessential features should be considered before the product's most important parts. For example, a product can be branded differently in different places; branding qualifies as an inessential function, for the most part. Edge cases – the uses that are least common – also represent less essential functionality, and they can be safely changed as well. But core product functionality should be the last thing that gets changed.

In situations where you find yourself chopping at the meat of a product, changing core functions, it may be more useful to release two separate products to fulfill each user group. Be careful, however, of providing so many separate releases that it becomes difficult to update, support, or deploy new features.

7.7. Conduct demographic research.

When you don't know how people will use your product in other areas of the world, of diffrent ages, or across experience levels, you have to figure it out. In 4.1.2, I referred to ethnographic research, which is what designers use to find out how people work with technology. Ethnographic research has considerable writing devoted to it, but it's worth closing this chapter with a summary.

Ethnographic research can take many forms. We can observe people using products, we can ask them to complete tasks in an isolated setting (similar in format to usability testing), or we can interview them.

RECRUITMENT.

Recruitment is often the most difficult part. Sometimes it involves tracking people down on the street and asking if they have some time to answer questions about the products that they use. With controlled interviews, it involves a more focused search, narrowing down by gender, age, experience level, or country of origin.

Either way, it's difficult to recruit qualified participants who will offer useful views about their use. Because it may require too much effort to do in-house, firms frequently outsource this process to dedicated recruiting companies, who call random candidates and pose surveys to determine whether they're a good fit for the study.

CONTEXTUAL INQUIRY.

The process of informally interviewing users when they're completing a real-world task is called **contextual inquiry**.

Contextual inquiry involves *observing* real-world use and *asking questions* about that use. Doing the latter disrupts the former. Questioning can take place either during or after observation, depending on the circumstances and what kind of observations are made. For example, if someone is visibly frustrated with a product, or about to commit an error, it may make sense to ask them about it midway through their use, to understand the process that led them there.

Seeing the user in a practical context gives a lot of ancillary information about their work. You learn about physical affordances, personal customizations, and environmental factors in a way that formal testing simply can't provide. Also, contextual inquiry makes the user feel much more comfortable than placing them in unfamiliar surroundings and asking them to complete predetermined tasks. While less scientifically accurate, it can give you a more grounded perspective at a lower cost.

The nature of observations can vary. For example, say you're figuring out how people in a different country, of a certain age range, use cell phones. Contextual inquiry can help: you go to

If you're interested in further pursuing these strains of research, check out Kim Goodwin, *Designing for the Digital Age* (Wiley) and Indi Young, *Mental Models* (Rosenfeld Media).

The US government has more writings on best practices in contextual inquiry: http://www. usability.gov/methods/analyze_current/learn/contextual.html .

More structured usability testing is discussed in 4.1.11.

Sections 4.1.8 through 4.1.10 discuss best practices in interviews with stakeholders and users.

that country, track down people in the street that are using a cell phone and fit your demographic profile, and ask them questions about what they use, how they use it, and what they'd like in an ideal setup. Developing a spreadsheet application, on the other hand, probably requires less wandering around city streets: go into an office and observe people working with spreadsheets; ask them about what works and what doesn't.

INTERVIEWS.

Interview the user about what technology they use, what value they gain from it, and why. What do they use? How did they choose that product initially? What software do they install on it? What are their most common tasks? How have they customized it? How do they deal with errors? If the product is hardware, in what ways has it worn down after use?

Explore edge cases as well as common ones. How have life-long experts customized their products? How have people with full-time investment in your kind of product adapted it for their use? How do intermediates use your product?

IN SHORT.

Great products are frequently made when someone decides to fill a need of their own that current tools can't provide. In that way, he's developing for himself, and releasing it in the hopes that it will serve others similarly. But products can also be intended for others, right from the start.

Before you begin to design, you need to know who you're developing for – and that's why research is such an important step in many projects.

Conclusion

Interaction design is an art and a craft. The emphasis of this book is more about the craft. Art is hard to discuss in a style guide, while discussing craft, engineering, and research is comparatively easy. Art changes by the day; craft is stable. Creative solutions fit new interaction models as soon as those models are created, but concepts like Fitts' Law and the grid system remain fresh. The focus of this book on theory and technique over style and tactics has been intentional.

It would be easy, but dangerous, to overthink the problems that this book discusses and make something that's boring, confining, and over-engineered; something that doesn't provoke surprise, wonder, and joy. It would be just as dangerous to ignore the relatively recent trend of products that target everyday interactions, and in a much more guided and friendly way than ever before. These products are slowly finding their way outside the home, into business and government. In all fields, it has become vital for developers and designers to understand the way that people experience things: to the user, the product is the interface, and the interface is the product.

Interface principles are useful only towards defining a framework, a starting point. And while a framework is helpful, and while it may lend itself to a feature-complete product, it doesn't yet make anything *whole*. The soul of the product isn't there yet. And while soul is the hardest part of a product to conceive and build, and nearly impossible to describe in text, any product without it is only partially complete.

By definition, this book is incomplete. But the ground left to cover is certainly the most interesting, for the sake of its novelty: products we can't conceive, in entirely new categories. Gestural interaction models. New ways to process, display, and share information.

Maybe someday, this book will have a companion volume that discusses the gasps we make when something delights us on a screen. Or the applause that follows the demonstration of a novel and beautiful solution. Or the Internet chatter about some new tool that someone made to scratch some itch of theirs. *That* would be a fitting conclusion. *Cadence & Slang* is meant to be a start.

Nick Disabato
Chicago, IL
August 2010

GLOSSARY.

B:

Reference

Affordance: Anything that allows a certain action to take place. Can be a physical object, a property of an object, or elements of an interface.

Baseline: A consistent vertical height to align every line of text, so that the text gains a visual rhythm and users (or readers) learn where to expect subsequent lines and elements. Baselines can apply to both print design and interactive layouts.

Behavior: A product's response to user input.

Completion Time: The amount of time that it takes to finish a task.

Control: Any element that triggers behavior through clicking, typing, or touching.

Data-Ink Ratio: The amount of ink (or pixels) devoted to expressing data, divided by the total amount of ink (or pixels) in the layout. The data-ink ratio should usually remain as close to 1 as possible.

Element: Anything that affects an interface, from text to graphics to buttons to form controls.

Error Rate: The number of errors that a user commits per path. Hopefully zero.

Experience: The sum of interactions during one's ownership of a product.

Flow: The mental state of appearing lost in one's activity. In interaction design, flow frequently occurs when involved in repetitions of a task.

Grid System: A consistent division of a layout into columns and/or rows, providing a framework to arrange content. In an interface's layout, the most common division is in columns.

Interaction: The sum of paths in a given relationship with a product, from when it's opened (or turned on, etc) until when it's closed (or turned off, etc).

Interface: The appearance and context of the product: its layout, platform, system, and hardware.

Language: How the product communicates to the user. Encompasses elements' appearance, layout, copy, and behavior.

Layout: The way that elements are arranged in relationship to one another.

Mapping: A connection between a series of related controls and a series of related behaviors.

Mode: Any kind of setting that a user can trigger to activate a different set of behaviors on an otherwise identical interface.

Natural Mapping: A mapping where controls follow the same order as behaviors.

Normative Context: The subservience of a product's language and interface to its platform and system.

Path: A chain of steps that complete a given task.

Pattern: A definition of a recurring problem; discussion of its essence and implications; and an abstracted, reusable, visually expressed design solution.

Pattern Language: A series of many interdependent patterns that express the common solutions of a product's design.

Pliant: When a control triggers behavior. Elements are frequently disabled to indicate that they shouldn't be triggered. Unpliant elements are often referred to as *ghosted*, because they are commonly tinted a light gray.

Platform: Usually an operating system, the product to which your product is subservient.

Product: Any software or hardware that affords use. (Infrastructure, like cables or network switches, doesn't qualify: it's a means to an end.)

Quasimode: A mode that requires conscious user input to activate and deactivate.

Repetition: A step, or small set of steps, conducted multiple times to perform a collection of similar tasks.

Rhythm: A repetition performed periodically and consistently for a long period of time.

State: The set of behaviors dictated by a mode. Modes must contain at least two states.

Step: A discrete action that triggers behavior. (Individual key presses are not steps, but keyboard shortcuts are steps.)

System: Usually a computer, console, or smartphone, the integrated set of products which comprise an interface.

Task: The desired outcome of one's interaction.

Transition: The behavior between two subsequent steps.

Usability Testing: Any method that quantitatively determines the usability of a product. Measured in terms of error rate, number of steps required, or completion time.

Books.

Christopher Alexander, *Notes on the Synthesis of Form* (Harvard Paperbacks), *The Timeless Way of Building*, and *A Pattern Language* (Oxford University Press): The original source of design patterns, to which section 2.6 of *Cadence & Slang* owes its debt. Christopher Alexander is an architect who created pattern languages as a means of designing and planning humane cities and buildings. Since then, the idea of modular, repurposable patterns has found its way into many other walks of life, from education to object-oriented programming to interface design.

Robert Bringhurst, *The Elements of Typographic Style* (Hartley & Marks): The inspiration for the format of *Cadence & Slang*, this book - part reference guide, part manifesto of the printed word - remains vital for anyone concerned with making readable, beautiful text, both on and off the computer screen.

Alan Cooper, *About Face* (Wiley): First published in 1995, this book provided the scaffolding for the craft of interaction design. It focuses considerably on similar topics in *Cadence & Slang*: namely, the way that elements are arranged, and the way that they behave from step to step. Many of the terms defined in *Cadence & Slang* were first coined here. It's currently in its third edition; make sure you acquire an updated copy.

Erich Gamma, Richard Helm, Ralph Johnson, and John Vlissides, *Design Patterns* (Addison-Wesley Professional): Applies Christopher Alexander's ideas to software development theory. This book is a good way to frame programmatic problems to make code more appropriate and reusable.

Kim Goodwin, *Designing for the Digital Age* (Wiley): Goodwin is top brass at Alan Cooper's company (see the above book), and her reference tome reflects their design process. Where Cooper more closely covered the rigor of behavior and layout, this provides deep insight into the research side of interaction design: how to recruit and interview users, how to synthesize findings in a team, and how to observe real-world use of products. This book is tremendously useful in organizations where contextual inquiry takes a front seat.

Per Mollerup, *Marks of Excellence* (Phaidon): A reference on the meaning and history behind various company logos. Useful for determining the meaning behind many symbols, and can provide inspiration for interfaces' iconography.

Don Norman, *The Design of Everyday Things* (Doubleday Business): A taut, concise overview of the way that the built environment can fit humans a little better. Discusses affordances, common errors, and natural mappings, and is accessible to laypersons.

Jef Raskin, *The Humane Interface* (Addison-Wesley Professional): One of the first books to discuss interaction design. Raskin was the first interface professional to work at Apple, during the dawn of the personal computer. Among many other topics, Raskin discusses modes at length, which was helpful in establishing my reasoning here.

Jennifer Tidwell, *Designing Interfaces* (O'Reilly): The original book of design patterns for interface design, this book helps to define common layouts and some behavior with more rigor and timely pertinence.

Edward Tufte, *The Visual Display of Quantitative Information, Envisioning Information, Visual Explanations,* and *Beautiful Evidence* (Graphics Press): This quartet of books - a fifth is to be added in the coming years - remains the undisputed source for quality in information display. More than any others, they elevated data to a craft, honed after considerable practice. Printed to a staggeringly high quality standard by Tufte himself, these stand among the most beautiful books ever to be printed - and they're quite economical to own. Essential for every time you're presented with a series of data and need some way to express it beautifully.

Body text is set in Feijoa and captions are set in National, both of which are by Kris Sowersby. The title, page numbers, chapter numbers, and running heads are set in Skopex Gothic by Andrea Tinnes. Chapter titles are set in Feijoa Display by Kris Sowersby. Greek text is set in Didot, designed by Ambroise Firmin-Didot and digitally released by Takis Katsoulidis and George Matthiopoulos of the Greek Font Society. Hebrew text is set in Adobe Hebrew by John Hudson. The cover's typeface is Zine Slab, designed by Ole Schäfer and issued by FontFont.

Colophon

Design advice came from Adrienne Canzolino, Abby Covert, Colleen Mavis Hill, Derek Moore, Justin Siddons, and Jake Thomas, each of whom helped to make *Cadence & Slang* a little bit prettier.

Edits came from Justin Skolnick, Liz Danzico, William Couch, Ruthie BenDor, Michael Disabato, Erin Jivoff Watson, Ian Lesperance, Todd vanGoethem, Stephen Swift, and Kevin Clair. Their assistance was invaluable in ensuring that I set forth the best possible arguments, and I'm eternally grateful for their generosity and time.

The photograph of Nick is by Joseph Mohan.

Additional assistance came from Anthony Zinni, Rosamund Lannin, Matthew Cronin, Andrew Huff, Charles Adler, Alex Micek, and Vitorio Miliano. Special thanks to New Wave Coffee of Logan Square in Chicago.

Cadence & Slang wouldn't exist in its physical form if not for the financial contributions of 258 generous people. Through a website called Kickstarter, US$12,207 was raised to pay for printing and shipping costs.

Thanks and much love to Adam De Witt, Adam Russell, Adam J. Saint, Adnan Ali, Adrienne Canzolino, Agnes Schliebitz-Ponthus, Aleksander Kiin, Alex Robb, Alex S. Kelly of ASK Design CSI, Amy Bucciferro, Amy Hoy, Anders Smith, Andres Freyria, Andrew Gilmartin, Andy Baio, Andy Coffey, Andy Farley, Andy Gupta, Anna Titcomb, Anna Washenko, Arul Isai Imran, Auren E. Kaplan, Austin B. Harvey, Aylin Selcukoglu, Ben Davidson, Ben Husmann, Ben Lister, Benjamin McKinney, Bill Bright, Bill Welense, Bob and Debbie Matusiak, Brad, Brad Dougherty, Brad Greenlee, Brian Leli, Brice Russ,

Kickstarter funds the ideas of writers, artists, and anyone else with enough passion to make great things. For more information on funding others' projects or starting your own, check out http://kickstarter.com.

C. Chad Warford, Michael & Roxann Disabato, Cal Henderson, Cameron Kenley Hunt, Carol Bourne, Casey Caplowe, CB, Chantal Coryell, Charles Adler, Charles Berret, Chris Campbell, Chris Noessel, Chris Quackenbush, Chris Stiles, Chris Weiss, Christoph Doblander, Cinchel & Kirstie, Claude Précourt, @ cjkihlbom, Colin J. Hill, Danielle Ongart, Dave LeCompte, Dave Stroup, David Fromant, David L. Kinney, David Murphy, David Schlossberg, David W. Riordan, Diana Kimball, Douglas E. Sherwood, Douglas Sellers, Dunstan Orchard, Edward Ocampo-Gooding, Eric Eberhardt, Eric Gelinas, Eric Schickli, Eric Stevens, Erica Gorochow, Erik Moe, Erin Jivoff Watson, Evan Kerrigan, Evan Spacht, Faisal N. Jawdat, Felix Jung, Flavio Diomede, Frank @frankieshakes Manno, Fred Pfeiffer, Fred Stutzman, Fredrik Ohlin, Gabriele Lana, George Terezakis, Göran Hagert, Gordon Withers, Henri Huttunen, Henry Birdseye, Hisham Abboud, Hugh Kennedy, Ian Lesperance, Jack Cheng, Jacob Reiff, Jadrian Miles, Jake Desaulniers, James Callan, James VanOsdol, Jan Lehnardt, Jana Lepon, Jason Crane, Jason Medeiros, Jason Winters, Jason Zopf, Jean-Marie Vallet, Jed Bowtell, Jeffrey Long, Jennifer Brook, Jerry Gennaria, Jiayong Ou, Jim Puls, Jina Bolton, Jocelyn Richard, Jochen Wolters, Joe Mako, Joe Marinaro, Joey W., John Hanauer, Jon Bell of lot23.com, Jon Buda, Jon Maloto, Jon Whipple, Jonathan Abbett, Jonathan Stark, Joseph Mohan, Josh Samuels, Joshua Blount, Joshua Noble, Justin Siddons, Justin Skolnick, Justin Stephenson, KarlSF, kastner, Katherine Merriam, Katy Sharrock, Keith Collins, Keith Mason, KevBurnsJr, Kevin Clair, Kim Ahlström, Kitt Hodsden, Kristen Hazard, Lance Cookson, Leah Williams, Lee Dale, Leigh Kelsey, Lenny Rachitsky, Liz Thompson, Louise Disabato, Lukas Mathis, Luke Crawford, Magera Moon Holton, Marc Escobosa, Margaret Rooney, Mark Dallman, Martin McClellan, Martin Sweeney, Martins Spilners, Mary Gerhart, Mary South, Masha Aptekar, Matt Hooks, Matt Puchlerz, Matt Thomas, Matthew H. Garber Esq., Matthew Irish, Matthew Mittelstadt (Tape), Matthew Shanley, Maurice Rabb, Maya Kuper, mcvmcv.net, Miguel Carvalhais, Mike Matz, Mike West, Nadia M. Gaya, Nelson Pavlosky, Nicholas Bendler, Nicholas Chen, Nick Cernis, Nick Nunns, Nick Richards, Noah Witherspoon, Pascal Hertleif, Patti Carlson, Paul Cooper, Paul DeBeasi, Paul Hammond, Paul Thompson, Peter Abrahamsen, Peter Bourgon, Phil Dokas, Phil Genera, Philip Karpiak, Rahmin Sarabi, Ralph E. Johnson, Rein Groot, Rekha Murthy, Rien Swagerman, Rob Bevan, Rob Loukotka, Rob Walsh, Robert Loerzel, Robert Oles, Robert Spigner, Rocky Jones, Rose, Ross Harmes, Ross Hays, Ruthie BenDor, Ryan Nielsen, Sarah

Crabtree, Sarah Morgan, Scott Baldwin, Scott Jackson, Thee Mr. Sei Jin Lee, Sharlene King, Sheeva, Simon Starr, Skip Baney, smallhadroncollider, Stefan Seiz, Steve Scaysbrook, Steven Buss, Steven Robertson, Steven Tan, StreamSend Email Marketing, Suneel Gupta, Teresa Lee, Terrell Russell, Tim Gleason, Tim Messer, Tobie Langel, Todd vanGoethem, Tom Hughes, Tony Meyer, Tracy Mehoke on behalf of Project Sarurun, tuxella, Tyler Brown, Veken Gueyikian, Victoria Pater, Vitorio Miliano, Wesley Lindamood, William Couch, William Lindley, Zoltan Csaki, and seven donors who wished to be anonymous.

ABOUT THE AUTHOR.

Nick Disabato is an interaction designer, photographer, and craft beer advocate who loves usability, empathy, enthusiastic yelling, and beautiful things. He lives underneath train tracks in a very large neighborhood in Chicago, and he has very curly hair. For more information, and to get in touch, his personal site is at http://nickd.org.

ABOUT THE ILLUSTRATOR.

Daniel Bogan is an Australian ex-pat living in San Francisco. During the day, he makes the Internet with his bare hands at a small, inconsequential photo sharing site called Flickr; at night he turns into a vampire. He interviews talented folks about their favored products at The Setup, http://usesthis.com, and his personal site is at http://waferbaby.com.